RAF, Dominion & Allied Squadrons at War:
Study, History and Statistics

COMPILED BY
Phil H. LISTEMANN

Drawings by Chris Thomas

PREFACE

The purpose of this study is to provide aviation historians and enthusiasts with a range of information relative to each of the Commonwealth squadrons that saw combat during World War II. Each record will comprise a short history, complete with illustrations and artwork, and accompanied by the following appendices:

Appendix I: Squadron Commanders and Flight Commanders
Appendix II: Major awards
Appendix III: Operational diary (number of sorties per month)
Appendix IV: Victory list
Appendix V: Aircraft losses on operations
Appendix VI: Aircraft losses in accidents
Appendix VII: Aircraft Serial numbers matching with individual letters (including mission totals for multi-engine aircraft)
Appendix VIII: Nominal roll (Captains only for bomber and seaplane units)
Appendix IX: Roll of Honour

Individual files will be constantly updated, when any fresh information comes to light. Additional information will be available for download, at no charge, on each squadron's site at:

www.RAF-IN-COMBAT.com

GLOSSARY OF TERMS

RANKS

AC: Aircraftman
G/C: Group Captain
W/C: Wing Commander
S/L: Squadron Leader
F/L: Flight Lieutenant
F/O: Flying Officer
P/O: Pilot Officer
W/O: Warrant Officer
F/Sgt: Flight Sergeant
Sgt: Sergeant
Cpl: Corporal
LAC: Leading Aircraftman

OTHER

AAF: Auxiliary Air Force
CO: Commanding Officer
DFC: Distinguished Flying Cross

DFM: Distinguished Flying Medal
DSO: Distinguished Service Order
Eva.: Evaded
Inj.: Injured
ORB: Operational Record Book
OTU: Operational Training Unit
PAF: Polish Air Force
PoW: Prisoner of War
RAF: Royal Air Force
RAAF: Royal Australian Air Force
RCAF: Royal Canadian Air Force
RNZAF: Royal New Zealand Air Force
SAAF: South African Air Force
Sqn: Squadron
TOC: Taken on charge
†: Killed

No. 137 Squadron 1941-1945

ISBN: 978-2-918590-60-6

Contributors & Acknowledgments:
Rob Bowater, John Gates, Hugh Halliday, John R. Nixon's family, Paul Sortehaug, Ken Smy, Andrew Thomas.

Cover: Westland Whirlwind P7012/SF-V, is re-armed with 250-lb bombs in May 1943.

MAIN EQUIPMENT

Whirlwind I	Sep.41 - Jun.43
Hurricane IV	Jun.43 - Jan.44
Typhoon I	Jan.44 - Aug.45

SQUADRON CODE LETTERS:

SF

SQUADRON HISTORY

1941 saw a big expansion with the RAF forming many squadrons. No.137 Squadron belongs to that category and was re-formed [1] on **20 September 1941** at Charmy Down, a satellite airfield of Colerne. Unlike the vast majority of day-fighter squadrons. which were formed on either Hurricane or Spitfire aircraft, No.137 Squadron was formed with Westland Whirlwind, being the second of only two operational units so equipped with this twin-engine machine.

By the end of September it had 18 Whirlwinds on charge, but only three pilots; more were posted in, mainly from the first Whirlwind unit, No.263 Squadron. As a consequence by 19 October No.137 Squadron was able to field one operational Flight. On 24 October the commanding officer, S/L John Sample, carried out the unit's first operational sortie along with Flying Officer Colin Clark, flying to Predannack to undertake an attack on fuel containers that had been reported in railway sidings at Landerneau, inland from Brest. After this tentative start to operations the squadron received a most unfortunate setback when, four days later, during practice interceptions, S/L Sample's Whirlwind was in collision with another flown by a new pilot, both being killed. The squadron became non-operational for a short period and resumed operations on the 10 November with sweeps and coastal patrols from East Anglia. A major loss came on 12 February 1942 when four Whirlwinds were tasked to escort destroyers, but were unable to locate the Allied ships. However, two battleships were sighted and, believing them to be friendly, the Whirlwind pilots investigated; it was a fatal error. They were no less than the *Scharnhorst* and *Gneisenau* making their famous 'Channel dash', with five or six destroyers and flak ships, and the Whirlwinds were immediately set upon by the Luftwaffe fighter escort, and all shot down. Despite an increasing number of operations with losses the squadron was unable to claim its first confirmed victory until 25 July 1942 when P/O John McClure and W/O Robert Smith shared the destruction of a Ju88. Two others victories were recorded before 137 Squadron switched to a fighter-bomber role, with its Whirlwinds being fitted with bomb racks. Despite shooting down a fourth enemy aircraft on the 19th December, the unit's activity was generally low, with just a small number of operations being carried out before the Whirlwinds were replaced by rocket-equipped Hurricane Mk.IV aircraft in June 1943. The first Hurricane sortie was carried out on 23 July, although the Hurricane era was a short-lived affair because in December No.137 Squadron began to convert to Hawker Typhoons, which became the last aircraft type it was to fly until the end of the war.

Its first Typhoon operation was on 8 February 1944, flying escort to bombers, and during the following weeks, the squadron began carrying out shipping reconnaissances and *Ramrods* with bombs, before receiving rocket-equipped machines in April. From that point, the number of sorties began to increase steadily under the command of a new CO, a Norwegian, Major Gunnar Piltinsgrud. No.137 Squadron remained under ADGB authority over the next few weeks, being one of only two Typhoon units in this Command at that time. In June 1944, it started its Army support work, and also carried out anti-shipping patrols. It was also involved in a non-planned task, the shooting down of V-1 flying bombs, which were being directed at the English capital. Between 22 June and 4 August 1944, 30 were shot down by its Typhoons, two pilots being particularly successful, F/L Douglas Brandbreth and the New Zealander F/L Arthur Sames. On 13 August, the squadron became part of 124 Wing, 2nd TAF on the Continent, equipped with its rocket-armed Typhoons. It travelled with the Wing through Belgium, Holland and finally into Germany where it was based at the end of the hostilities. During this period, the unit registered its fifth and last air victory (V-1s aside) on 31 December 1944, when P/O Richard Egley shot down a Fw190. Its last sorties were carried out on 4 May 1945. No.137 Squadron remained stationed in Germany until August 1945 when it returned to the UK to be disbanded on the **25 August 1945**, and re-numbered No.174 Squadron. In 4 years the squadron suffered quite a heavy toll, losing 45 pilots killed during some 6,100 sorties. Another eight flying personnel became prisoners.

[1] No.137 Sqn was first formed in April 1918 but never became operational and was disbanded in July the same year.

SQUADRON BASES

Charmy Down	20.09.41 - 08.11.41	Amiens-Glisy/B-48 (France)	03.09.44 - 06.09.44
Coltishall	08.11.41 - 01.12.41	Melsbroek/B-58 (Belgium)	06.09.44 - 23.09.44
Matlask	01.12.41 - 24.08.42	Eindhoven/B-78 (Netherlands)	23.09.44 - 13.01.45
Snailwell	24.08.42 - 17.09.42	Helmond/B-86 (Netherlands)	13.01.45 - 07.03.45
Manston	17.09.42 - 12.06.43	Warmwell	07.03.45 - 19.03.45
Southend	12.06.43 - 08.08.43	Helmond/B-86 (Netherlands)	19.03.45 - 11.04.45
Manston	08.08.43 - 14.12.43	Twente/B-106 (Netherlands)	11.04.45 - 14.04.45
Lympne	14.12.43 - 02.01.44	Hopsten/B-112 (Germany)	14.04.45 - 17.04.45
Colerne	02.01.44 - 23.01.44	Langenhagen/B-120 (Germany)	17.04.45 - 01.05.45
Fairwood Common	23.01.44 - 04.02.44	Lüneburg/B-156 (Germany)	01.05.45 - 07.05.45
Lympne	04.02.44 - 01.04.44	Celle/B-118 (Germany)	07.05.45 - 09.05.45
Manston	01.04.44 - 14.08.44	Kastrup/B-160 (Denmark)	09.05.45 - 21.06.45
Coulombs/B-6 (France)	14.08.44 - 28.08.44	Husum/B-172 (Germany)	21.06.45 - 11.07.45
Créton/B-30 (France)	28.08.44 - 03.09.44	Lübeck/B-158 (Germany)	11.07.45 - 20.08.45
		Warmwell	20.08.45 - 26.08.45

APPENDIX I
SQUADRON AND FLIGHT COMMANDERS

Rank and Name	SN	Origin	Dates
S/L John **SAMPLE** (†)	AAF No.90278	RAF	20.09.41 - 28.10.41
S/L Humphrey St.J. **COGHLAN**	AAF No.90117	RAF	01.11.41 - 20.05.43
S/L John B. **WRAY**	RAF No.37874	RAF	20.05.43 - 05.12.43
S/L John R. **DENNEHAY**	RAF No.102538	RAF	05.12.43 - 24.04.44
Maj. Gunnar **PILTINGSRUD** (†)	RAF No.N.1087	RNAF	24.04.44 - 24.09.44
S/L Erle T. **BROUGH**	NZ412197	RNZAF	27.09.44 - 08.12.44
S/L Ronald G.V. **BARRACLOUGH**	RAF No.66487	RAF	26.12.44 - 27.03.45
S/L Douglas **MURRAY**	RAF No.119128	RAF	30.03.45 - 25.08.45

A FLIGHT

Rank and Name	SN	Origin	Dates
F/L Joseph G. **HUGHES**	RAF No.41706	RAF	22.09.41 - 16.12.41
F/L Guy **MARSLAND**	RAF No.41940	RAF	16.12.41 - 18.02.42
F/L Joseph W.E. **HOLMES**	RAF No.114291	RAF	18.02.42 - 16.02.43
F/L John M. **BRYAN**	RAF No.102570	RAF	16.02.43 - 31.08.43
F/L Idwal J. **DAVIES**	RAF No.63418	RAF	31.08.43 - 30.11.43
F/L Ronald E.G. **SHEWARD**	RAF No.120531	(ARG)/RAF	01.12.43 - 01.05.44
F/L Harold C. **KNIGHT** (†)	RAF No.80270	(SA)/RAF	01.05.44 - 21.05.44
F/L Ralph A. **JOHNSTONE**	CAN./J.22310	RCAF	21.05.44 - 21.06.44
F/L Clifford R. **ABBOTT**	CAN./J.17953	RCAF	21.06.44 - 10.09.44
F/L Walker H.B. **SHORT**	RAF No.136419	RAF	10.09.44 - 01.12.44
F/L John L. **CROSSLEY** (PoW)	RAF No.100647	RAF	01.12.44 - 29.12.44
F/L George **CLUBLEY**	RAF No.174402	RAF	31.12.44 - 18.03.45
Capt James I.A. **WATT**	SAAF No.328515	SAAF	18.03.45 - 25.08.45

B FLIGHT

Rank and Name	SN	Origin	Dates
F/L Colin A.G. **CLARKE**	RAF No.42192	(SA)/RAF	??.09.41 - 30.10.41
F/L Robert S. **WOODWARD**	RAF No.74698	RAF	07.11.41 - 12.02.42
F/L John E. **VAN SHAICK**	RAF No.114086	RAF	12.02.42 - 01.12.42
F/L Alexander **TORRANCE**	RAF No.64932	RAF	03.12.42 - 05.10.43
F/L John **LONDON**	RAF No.115148	RAF	13.10.43 - 07.05.44
F/L Douglas G. **BRANDRETH**	RAF No.155460	RAF	07.05.44 - 01.11.44
F/L Peter E. **TICKNER**	RAF No.121411	RAF	02.11.44 - 05.01.45
F/L John **RENDALL**	AUS.413663	RAAF	13.01.45 - 22.04.45
F/L Dennis O. **LUKE**	RAF No.124524	RAF	22.04.45 - 25.08.45

APPENDIX II
MAJOR AWARDS

DSO: -

DFC: 12
*including 1 Bar: ***
Joel Hilton **ASHTON** (CAN./17890 - RCAF)
Kenneth George **BRAIN** (No.171047 - RAF)
Arthur Gaston **BRUNET** (CAN./17907 - RCAF)
John Michael **BRYAN** (No.102570 - RAF)
John Michael **BRYAN** (No.102570 - RAF)*
Michael James Burke **COLE** (No.156033 - RAF)
Joseph Laurier **DEHOUX** (CAN./15145 - RCAF)
Richard Akehurst **EGLEY** (NZ421690 - RNZAF)
John Edward **McCLURE** (CAN./15505 - RCAF)
Edward Lancelot **MUSGRAVE** (AUS.403528 - RAAF)
Walter Horace Bruce **SHORT** (No.136419 - RAF)
Mark John **WHITBY** (AUS.413056 - RAAF)

DFM: 1
Aubrey Cartwright **SMITH** (No.1340628 - RAF)

APPENDIX III
OPERATIONAL DIARY
NUMBER OF SORTIES PER MONTH

Date	Month	Total	Date	Month	Total
Oct.41	6	6	Oct.43	54	2,375
Nov.41	75	81	Nov.43	30	2,405
Dec.41	149	230	Dec.43	92	2,497
Jan.42	114	344	Jan.44	-	2,497
Feb.42	213	557	Feb.44	95	2,592
Mar.42	105	662	Mar.44	83	2,675
Apr.42	189	851	Apr.44	69	2,744
May.42	255	1,106	May.44	205	2,949
Jun.42	195	1,301	Jun.44	392	3,341
Jul.42	245	1,546	Jul.44	432	3,773
Aug.42	110	1,656	Aug.44	231	4,004
Sep.42	22	1,678	Sep.44	410	4,414
Oct.42	52	1,730	Oct.44	367	4,781
Nov.42	54	1,784	Nov.44	193	4,974
Dec.42	72	1,856	Dec.44	175	5,149
			Jan.45	120	5,269
Jan.43	59	1,915	Feb.45	260	5,529
Feb.43	47	1,962	Mar.45	215	5,744
Mar.43	52	2,014	Apr.45	307	6,051
Apr.43	87	2,101	May.45	107	6,158
May.43	67	2,168			
Jun.43	55	2,223	**Grand Total**		**6,158**
Jul.43	10	2,233			
Aug.43	43	2,276	Extracted from AIR27/954		
Sep.43	45	2,321			

APPENDIX IV
VICTORY LIST
CONFIRMED (C) AND PROBABLE (P) CLAIMS

Date	Pilot	SN	Origin	Type	Serial	Code	Nb	Cat.
		WHIRLWIND I						
25.07.42	P/O John E. **McClure**	Can./J.15505	RCAF	Ju88	**P7104**		0.5	C
	W/O Robert L. **Smith**	RAF No.742902	RAF		**P7102**	SF-P	0.5	C
29.07.42	F/Sgt James R. **Rebbetoy**	Can./R.75651	RCAF	Ju88	**P7058**	SF-G	0.5	C
	Sgt Leo **O'Neill**	RAF No530323	RAF		**P7005**	SF-H	0.5	C
19.08.42	F/O John M. **Bryan**	RAF No.102570	RAF	Do217	**P7121**	SF-C	0.5	C
	Sgt Desmond A. **Roberts**	NZ411994	RNZAF		**P7046**		0.5	C
19.12.42	F/O John M. **Bryan**	RAF No.102570	RAF	Fw190	**P7114**		0.5	C
	P/O James R. **Rebbetoy**	Can./J.15741	RCAF		**P7005**	SF-H	0.5	C
		TYPHOON I						
22.06.44	P/O Kenneth G. **Brain**	RAF No.171047	RAF	V-1	**MN191**	SF-P	2.0	C
	F/L Douglas G. **Brandreth**	RAF No.155460	RAF	V-1	**MN584**	SF-U	1.0	C
	W/O John A. **Horne**	Aus.405973	RAAF	V-1	**MN627**	SF-N	1.0	C
26.06.44	F/O Arthur N. **Sames**	NZ411453	RNZAF	V-1	**MN134**	SF-S	2.0	C
28.06.44	W/O John A. **Horne**	Aus.405973	RAAF	V-1	**MN429**	SF-B	0.5	C
	F/Sgt Laurence A.V. **Burrows**	RAF No.958745	RAF		**MN351**	SF-D	0.5	C
30.06.44	F/O Noel J.M. **Manfred**	Aus.413627	RAAF	V-1	**MN596**	SF-Q	1.0	C
	F/O Ralph A. **Johnstone**	Can./J.22310	RCAF	V-1	**MN152**	SF-T	1.0	C
	P/O Kenneth G. **Brain**	RAF No.171047	RAF	V-1	**MN169**	SF-J	1.5	C
	F/L Matthew **Wood**	Can./J.5540	RCAF		**MN134**	SF-S	0.5	C
05.07.44	F/O James C. **Holder**	Can./J.25779	RCAF	V-1	**MN584**	SF-U	1.0	C
	P/O Henry T. **Nicholls**	RAF No.174073	RAF	V-1	**MN134**	SF-S	1.0	C
06.07.44	W/C Gordon L. **Raphael**	RAF No.37508	(CAN)/RAF	V-1	**MN134**	SF-S	1.0	C
07.07.44	F/L Matthew **Wood**	Can./J.5540	RCAF	V-1	**MN627**	SF-N	1.0	C
	F/Sgt Lewis P. **Boucher**	RAF No.658691	RAF	V-1	**MN152**	SF-T	1.0	C
	F/O Ralph A. **Johnstone**	Can./J.22310	RCAF	V-1	**MN134**	SF-S	1.0	C
	F/O David W. **Guttridge**	RAF No.150045	RAF	V-1	**MN169**	SF-J	1.0	C
	P/O Henry T. **Nicholls**	RAF No.174073	RAF	V-1	**MN198**	SF-L	1.0	C
	F/O James C. **Holder**	Can./J.25779	RCAF	V-1	**MN627**	SF-N	2.0	C
09.07.44	F/L Douglas G. **Brandreth**	RAF No.155460	RAF	V-1	**MN134**	SF-S	1.0	C
13.07.44	F/O Arthur N. **Sames**	NZ411453	RNZAF	V-1	**MN134**	SF-S	1.0	C
26.07.44	F/O James C. **Holder**	Can./J.25779	RCAF	V-1	**MN134**	SF-S	2.0	C
29.07.44	F/L Douglas G. **Brandreth**	RAF No.155460	RAF	V-1	**MN198**	SF-L	1.0	C
30.07.44	F/O Noel J.M. **Manfred**	Aus.413627	RAAF	V-1	**MN169**	SF-J	1.0	C
03.08.44	F/L Douglas G. **Brandreth**	RAF No.155460	RAF	V-1	**MN198**	SF-L	1.0	C
04.08.44	F/O Arthur N. **Sames**	NZ411453	RNZAF	V-1	**MN134**	SF-S	1.0	C
31.12.44	P/O Richard A. **Egley**	NZ421690	RNZAF	Fw190	**MN198**	SF-L	1.0	C

Total: 5.0 aircraft & 30 V-1s

Aircraft damaged: 14

APPENDIX V
AIRCRAFT LOST ON OPERATIONS

Date	Pilot	S/N	Origin	Serial	Code	Mark	Fate

WHIRLWIND

30.10.41   F/O Colin A.G. **CLARK**   RAF No.42192   (SA)/RAF   **P7091**   I   †
Took off from Predannack with Sgt Douglas Jowitt at 09.40 for a 'Mandolin' operation. The Channel was crossed at 50 feet and landfall was made at Pontsuval. Attacks were made from 300 feet by both aircraft on trucks and many were hits seen. On the return journey Sgt Jowitt overtook F/O Clark who was seen to be flying on one engine. Jowitt called up F/O Clark on the radio but was unable to understand his reply. Sgt Jowitt climbed to 1,500 feet to weave around F/O Clark but did not find him. Being short petrol, Jowitt returned to Predannack safely at 11.10. Colin Clark seems to have made an emergency landing on water and was picked up by a destroyer where he died from injuries sustained during the crash. Colin Clark was a South African native of Transvaal. He had joined the RAF on a SSC in April 1939 and had served with the FIU during the Battle of Britain.
Note on the aircraft: TOC No.51 MU 08.07.41, issued to No.137 Sqn 22.09.41.

10.11.41   F/Sgt Basil L. **ROBERTSON**   RAF No.748333   RAF   **P6977**   I   -
Took off at 12.10 to patrol base in company of a Spitfire. After ten minutes the pair were recalled due to very bad weather and accompanying low ceiling, and pilot crashed on landing. Basil Roberston had been posted the previous month from No.263, with whom he had served just a few days. (see also entry 12.02.42)
Note on the aircraft: TOC direct No.263 Sqn 07.11.40, issued to No.137 Sqn 01.11.41.

12.02.42   P/O Ralph O.G. **HÄGGBERG**   RAF No.120677   (SWE)/RAF **P7106**   SF-D I   †
Took off at 13.10 with three others to provide cover for 5 destroyers attempting to intercept the Scharnhorst *and* Gneisenau. *Attacked by four Bf109s about 20 miles from the Belgian Coast and was shot down in the ensuing combat. Posted in October 1941 from No.263 Sqn, with which he had served since mid-September. Partly educated in England where his father was working. When war broke he was back in Sweden and returned to the UK in October 1939 to enlist in the RAF. As he was born in 1922 he was not accepted until December 1940, by which time he had turned 18. One of just a few Swedes to enlist in the RAF during the war.*
Note on the aircraft: TOC No.51 MU 30.08.41, issued to No.137 Sqn 20.09.41.

              W/O Basil L. **ROBERTSON**   RAF No.748333   RAF   **P7050**   I   †
See above. Basil Roberston had been posted the previous month from No.263, with whom he had served just a few days.
Note on the aircraft: TOC No.18 MU 24.05.41, issued to No.137 Sqn 28.09.41.

              Sgt John A.W. **SANDY**   RAF No.1051978 RAF   **P7107**   I   †
See above. Posted from No.263 Sqn in which he served only a few days. Commissioned three days earlier, as 116508, but was still wearing his Sergeant badges when lost.
Note on the aircraft: TOC No.51 MU 30.08.41, issued to No.137 Sqn 20.09.41.

              P/O George W. **MARTIN**   RAF No.102619   RAF   **P7093**   SF-A I   †
See above. George Martin joined the Squadron in October 1941 having been posted from No.263 Sqn, in which he served only a few days.
Note on the aircraft: TOC No.51 MU 17.07.41, issued to No.137 Sqn 17.01.42.

27.05.42   F/Sgt John R. **BRENNAN**   CAN./R.72637   RCAF   **P7122**   I   †
Took off at 09.40 for an Outer Channel patrol with P/O Paul La Gette (USA). At 10,000 feet they intercepted a Ju88, which was

to escape. However John Brennan did not report back to base, the last contact with him occurring at the beginning of the return journey. A Canadian native of Prince Edward Island, he had served in the squadron since November 1941.

Note on the aircraft: TOC No.39 MU 16.12.41, issued to No.137 Sqn 13.03.42. Last Whirlwind built. FH: 93.0.

29.05.42   P/O Douglas St-J. **Jowitt**   RAF No.114169   RAF   **P7118**   I   -

Took off at 05.20 for an early patrol with F/Sgt 'Ash' Ashton. During the return flight was forced to bale near Sheringham out when his port engine caught fire at 800 feet and the Whirlwind went into a spin. Had joined the squadron late in 1941, having served previously with No.263 Sqn between January and October 1941. (See also entry 31.10.42)

Note on the aircraft: TOC No.39 MU 11.11.41, issued to No.137 Sqn 20.02.42. FH:111.0.

27.06.42   P/O Frederick M. **Furber**   RAF No.80203   (RHO)/RAF   **P7049**   I   -

Took off at 21.30 for an evening patrol with F/O AlexanderTorrance. Caught fire probably due to glycol leak and abandond near Sheringham, Norfolk. Having joined the squadron in March 1942, he was posted to No.266 (Rhodesia) Sqn in January 1943, he was later shot down and made PoW on 09.07.43 (Typhoon R8804).

Note on the aircraft: TOC No.39 MU 23.05.41, issued to No.137 Sqn 22.09.41.

31.10.42   F/L John E. **van Schaick**   RAF No.114086   RAF   **P7064**   I   -

Took off at 11.00 with three others for a RHUBARB operation, John van Schaick leading. He and his wingman, Sgt Francis Waldron, attacked a hutted camp near Etampes (France). He was forced to ditch his aircraft in the sea off Boulogne, later being picked up by a Walrus. John van Schaick left the Squadron soon after as his tour expired. He had joined the squadron in February 1942, posted from No.609 Sqn in which he had served between September 1941 and February 1942, and had previously flown with No.266 Sqn between November 1940 and September 1941. Posted as an instructor to No.59 OTU, he was killed in a flying accident on 20.02.43 (Master T8533). He was credited with two confirmed victories with Nos.266 and 609 Sqn and was awarded a DFM [No.609 Sqn].

Note on the aircraft: TOC No.51 MU 02.07.41, issued to No.137 Sqn 18.11.41.

Sgt Francis G. **Waldron**   RAF No.1277168   RAF   **P7109**   I   **PoW**

See above. Did not return to base, cause unknown. Later reported a PoW at Stalag Luft VI.

Note on the aircraft: TOC No.51 MU 10.09.41, issued to No.137 Sqn 15.11.41.

P/O Douglas St-J. **Jowitt**   RAF No.114169   RAF   **P7115**   I   †

See above. Hit by ground fire while searching for the target, causing white smoke trailing from his starboard engine. Upon crossing the French coast, his wingman P/O Frederick Furber, called a mayday at Jowitt's request, as he was preparing to abandon the aircraft. Unfortunately nothing further was heard of him again. P/O Furber was the only one of the four to return from this operation. (see also entry 29.05.42).

Note on the aircraft: TOC No.39 MU 13.10.41, issued to No.137 Sqn 16.09.42.

22.12.42   Sgt Thomas A. **Sutherland**   RAF No.655932   RAF   **P6998**   I   -

Took off at 11.25 for RHUBARB operation around Abbeville (France) with F/O Edward Musgrave (RAAF) who was leading. They found a goods train stationed at a small station and both dropped their 250 lb bombs on it. At that moment Sutherland was hit by flak that was coming from each side of the station. Suffering strikes in the starboard engine and through the port cowling he set course to base. However one engine seized before the English coast was reached and he crash-landed at Lympne. Sutherland had joined the squadron during the Autumn.

Note on the aircraft: TOC direct No.263 Sqn 23.02.41. Issued to No.137 Sqn 13.09.42.

17.01.43   P/O John F. **Luing**   RAF No.121527   RAF   **P7051**   I   -

Took off at 01.22 from Ford with for an intruder operation. While taking off his Whirlwind hit a hole causing a wing-tip to touch the ground. The aircraft caught fire, and 'Jack' Luing was able to escape from it before the bombs exploded. He started his flying career with a University Air Squadron at Derby. Called up at the outbreak of WWII he found himself at No.604 Sqn, with which he served until October 1941, passing very briefly through 263 Sqn before joining 137 Sqn that same month. In August 1942 he was posted to HQFC, for liaison duties with USAAF, flying Lockheed Lightnings. Back to No.137 Sqn until September 1943 when he was posted to India, eventually joining No.211 Sqn in January 1944 flying Beaufighter Xs. Shot down and captured by the Japanese on 8 March 1944 (Beaufighter LZ364), he later died in captivity on 24 October 1944.

Note on the aircraft: TOC No.18 MU 02.06.41, issued to No.137 Sqn 18.10.42. Previously served with No.263 Sqn.

23.01.43	W/O Alec I. **Doig**	RAF No.565057	RAF	**P7054**		I	**PoW**

Took of for a RHUBARB at 10.55. Dropped 2 x 250 lb bomb on a goods train, about half a mile N of Neufchatel, hitting some of the trucks. The train was then attacked with cannon, strikes being seen on trucks and the engine. Another goods train of about 50 trucks, was attacked near Sergeux with strikes being observed on both engine and trucks. The section returned then to Neufchatel where an engine in the station was attacked, steam being seen issuing from sides. P/O John McClure (RCAF) and Doing encountered intense light flak when over Poperinge, forcing the two to split, after which no further news was had of Doing. He was later reported a PoW.

Note on the aircraft: TOC No.39 MU No.17.06.41. Issued to No.137 Sqn 23.09.42. Served at various times with No.263 and No.137 Sqn in 1942.

	Sgt Alfred E. **Brown**	RAF No.646417	RAF	**P7095**	SF-H	I	†

Took off 10.55 for a RHUBARB sortie, Lt Norman Freeman (SAAF) leading. Attacked with cannon a goods train waiting outside of Aubigny station, the engine being left enveloped in steam. They then found a goods train of 45 trucks, N. of Doullens, on which they dropped their 2 x 250 lb bombs. The engine, which was pouring steam, and the first five coaches, were derailed and left lying on their sides. Light flak was experienced from the centre of the train and the pair lost each other in cloud. Sgt Brown contacted Lt Freeman on the R/T and told him he was okay, but believed he had been hit in the port engine. Commissioned a few days earlier, as 141474, but was still wearing Sergeant stripes when lost.

Note on the aircraft: TOC No.51 MU 21.07.41, issued to No.137 Sqn 22.06.42.

19.02.43	P/O Charles E. **Mercer**	Can./J.15738	RCAF	**P7114**		I	†

At 01.10, whilst taking-off on an Intruder operation, due to a misunderstanding, Mercer crashed into Neville Freeman's aircraft as it was taxiing on to the flarepath at Manston. Both machines caught fire and 2 bombs exploded. A Canadian, native of Nova Scotia, he arrived in UK in March 1941 and had served in the squadron since October 1941.

Note on the aircraft: TOC No.39 MU 29.09.41, issued to No.137 Sqn 17.11.42. Served previously with No.263 Sqn.

	Lt Neville A. **Freeman**	SAAF No.19862	SAAF	**P7119**		I	†

See above. A South African, native of Cape Town, he had served in the squadron since March 1942.

Note on the aircraft: TOC No.48 MU 11.11.41, issued to No.137 Sqn 08.03.42.

02.03.43	Sgt George O.H. **Walker**	RAF No.1382117	RAF	**P7005**	SF-H	I	**PoW**

Took off 13.10 with 2 others, S/L Humphrey Coghan leading, to attack railways targets in the Neufchatel area. The trio were forced to return after making a brief landfall as cloud-base was down to hilltop level. W/O Arthur Brunet (RCAF) lost Sgt Walker in cloud, who asked for a vector home. Walker indicated that he was Ok but when Brunet was near the English coast he heard the former give a Mayday, which was not picked up by the ground station. Searches were made by Brunet, P/O 'Jack' Luing and W/O 'Ash' Ashton (RCAF), with no success. Walker was later reported PoW at Stalag 344.

Note on the aircraft: TOC No.39 MU 03.04.41, issued to No.137 Sqn 08.03.42. Served previously with No.263 Sqn.

04.04.43	P/O Norbury **Dugdale**	RAF No.131147	RAF	**P7002**	SF-W	I	-

Took off at 08.30 with 7 others for a shipping patrol, the CO leading. An escort, in the form of 9 Typhoons, was provided. On the way out Dugdale flying with the formation at sea level, hit the sea with his props, tried to gain height unsuccessfully, and ditched his Whirlwind 5 miles off Dungeness. He got clear of the aircraft and was picked up, after about 5 minutes in the water, by a sea rescue launch that was patrolling in the area. Dugdale had joined the squadron the previous month, having served very briefly in No.611 Sqn.

Note on the aircraft: TOC direct No.263 Sqn 13.03.41, issued to No.137 Sqn 02.02.43. FH; 278.0

25.04.43   F/O James R. **REBBETOY**   CAN./J.15741   RCAF   **P7058**   SF-G   I   †

Took off at 10.35 with 5 others for Rhubarb mission. He was No.2 to F/L 'Mike' Bryan, who was leading the formation. They were about to attack a train, with 5 coaches near Thielt, when F/L Bryan observed flak from the coaches. He broke away and told Rebbetoy over the R/T not to attack, but immediately afterwards saw his No.2 beating up the train with cannon, and noticed strikes on the engine and first truck. A little later he saw an explosion with flames and smoke in a field in the vicinity, which was believed to be Rebbetoy's machine. A Canadian, native of Ontario, he had served in the squadron since November 1941.

Note on the aircraft: TOC No.18 MU 22.06.41, issued to No.137 Sqn 25.09.41. FH: 320.6

17.05.43   F/O Edward L. **MUSGRAVE**   AUS.403528   RAAF   **P7063**   I   †

Took off alone at 01.10 to attack shipping in the Gravelines area. He was plotted at 01.32, by the C.H.L. Station, attacking ships, but then the plot disappeared and no further news was received of him. An Australian from New South Wales, who had been in the squadron for 18 months.

Note on the aircraft: TOC No.39 MU 22.06.41, issued to No.137 Sqn 16.03.42. Previously served with No.263 Sqn.

HURRICANE

14.08.43   P/O John T. **DAVIDSON**   RAF No.114577   RAF   **KZ578**   IV   †

Took off at 22.35 for an anti-shipping patrol and, on his way back, at 23.25 was mistaken for an enemy, by a Mosquito, and inadvertently shot down about 10 miles off N. Foreland. The aircraft was seen to come down in flames and, although a search of the area was made, no trace of the pilot could be found. 'Dave' Davidson had joined the squadron in March.

Note on the aircraft: TOC No.48 MU 14.04.43, issued to No.137 Sqn 15.06.43.

17.08.43   F/O Philip H.B. **UNWIN**   RAF No.111127   RAF   **KW918**   SF-C   IV   -

Took off at 0133 with F/O Bernard Soulsby for an anti-shipping patrol and became lost. After several vectors, and being airborne for two hours, he had just reached the English coast, when his petrol gave out. He attempted to land at Manston but crash-landed about 200 yards short. Unwin had been with the squadron two months, and in December was posted to No.164 Sqn.

Note on the aircraft: TOC No.41 MU 23.05.43, issued to No.137 Sqn 17.06.43.

02.09.43   F/O Joseph L. **DEHOUX**   CAN./J.15145   RCAF   **KX698**   SF-F   IV   †

Took off at 09.15 with 3 others, S/L Wray leading, in company of 8 Hurricanes of 164 Sqn to destroy lockgates at Hansweert. An escort was provided by Typhoons of Nos.3 and 198 Sqns. The coast was crossed east of Knocker, and Dehoux was seen to fire his rockets at the target and pull away, after which no further news was received of him. A Canadian, native of Province of Quebec, he had been with the squadron for nearly 2 years. Trained in Canada, he arrived in UK in March 1941. His brother, J.F.G.R. Dehoux, an air gunner with No.419 (RCAF) Sqn, was also killed in action, on 20 February 1944.

Note on the aircraft: TOC No.22 MU 06.02.43, issued to No.137 Sqn 29.06.43. FH:58.7.

14.09.43   F/O Hugh G. **DICKSON**   CAN./J.26498   RCAF   **KZ656**   IV   †

Took off at 23.05 for anti-shipping patrol, and last heard of about 12 miles off Ostende (Belgium) at 23.45. A Canadian, native of Nova Scotia, he served in Canada with No.118 (F) Sqn, RCAF, from April 1941 until being sent to the UK in June 1943. He had joined the squadron during July.

Note on the aircraft: TOC No.22 MU 27.04.43, issued to No.137 Sqn 01.09.43. FH:17.6.

07.10.43   F/O Bernard **SOULSBY**   RAF No.127729   RAF   **KZ620**   SF-X   IV   †

Took off at 06.50 with 7 others, F/L Idwal Davies leading, to attack any shipping that might be found between Walcheren and Noord Beveland Islands. An escort was provided by No.198 Sqn Typhoons. The Hurricanes, flying at sea level, made landfall at the south-west corner of Schouwen Island, but the Typhoons engaged three Fw190s and did not arrive. Because the cloud base was down to 1,200 ft, F/L Davies decided that the Hurricanes could continue alone. As the formation was turning to starboard Soulsby was seen to straighten out and then crash into the sea, debris flying up. When F/Sgt Nickless flew back over the spot he could see no sign of anything on the water. Bernard Soulsby had been in the squadron since April.

Note on the aircraft: TOC No.22 MU 27.05.43, issued to No.137 Sqn 22.06.43. FH:116.6.

TYPHOON

12.02.44   P/O Jack W.T. **PURDY**   RAF No.169567   RAF   **MM974**   SF-R   IB   †

Took off at 14.00 with 9 others, led by S/L Dennehey, for RAMROD 548. Light flight was encountered. Approximately 3-5 minutes after arrival in target area a call from P/O 'Jack' Purdy, 'Red 3', was heard saying that his engine was cutting and that he probably have to put down. This was the last contact received from pilot, who had joined the squadron the previous month. He was last seen near Ardouval.

Note on the aircraft:TOC No.20 MU 22.12.43, issued to No.137 Sqn 14.01.44. FH:14.0

01.04.44   W/O John W. **CARTER**   Aus.412912   RAAF   **MN145**   SF-B   IB   †

Scrambled at 22.00 for a shipping patrol, covering area between Dunkirk and Flushing. Soon after commencement of patrol, Swingate control reported the plot faded and lost its trace. 'Skull' Carter was and Australian from New South Wales and had served with the squadron since August 43. It was his first operational posting.

Note on the aircraft: TOC No.51 MU 06.01.44, issued to No.137 Sqn 27.03.44 from No.56 Sqn.

05.05.44   F/Sgt Reginald J. **EASTABROOK**   RAF No.1339249   RAF   **MM980**   SF-W   IB   †

Took off at 05.30 with 3 others, CO S/L Piltingsgrud leading. Two aircraft had RPs, and two were acting as fighter escort. The sweep extended from Ostend up to the Hook of Holland. Four trawlers were sighted 4 miles off the Hague, the CO positioning himself to attack the first ship, but the second RP aircraft (F/O RW Clarke) didn't hear the order and fell behind. 'Red' 1 released his salvo, but misjudged the range, and the rockets fell short. The second aircraft (F/S Reginald Estabrook) flew into the spray and was also hit by the ship's flak. He crashed into the water at 06.10. Estabrook had been with the squadron since August 1943, having been posted from No.164 Sqn, with which he briefly served.

Note on the aircraft: TOC No.51 MU 31.12.43, issued to No.137 Sqn 30.04.44 from No.56 Sqn.

21.05.44   F/O Arthur **HAWKER**   RAF No.135734   RAF   **MN312**   SF-J   IB   †

Took off at 06.58 for a shipping recce with W/O C.G. Points (Pink 2), F/O A. Hawker leading as 'Pink 1'. They patrolled Calais to Flushing, 2-3 miles off shore at deck level. Seeing no ships they turned for home. F/O Hawker turned into cloud and crossed the coast 3 miles west of Ostende, at 1,000 feet, F/Sgt Points following. Just after Pink 1 had asked for a homing from control the pair came under fire from the ground, and 'Pink 1' was hit crashing into the sea off Ostende (Belgium). Pilot had served in the squdron since January.

Note on the aircraft: TOC No.51 MU 22.02.44, issued to No.137 Sqn 22.03.44.

F/L Harold C. **KNIGHT**   RAF No.80270   (SA)/RAF   **JR433**   SF-T   IB   †

Took off at 10.25 with 7 other aircraft, four with RPs, and four acting as fighter cover, the CO leading. A goods train was attacked south of Thielt (Belgium) and F/L Knight, leading the second section, was hit by flak and his aircraft was seen to blow up, during a force-landing attempt. The mission continued and two other trains, a goods and a troop train, were attacked. The rest of the formation landed at base at 11.35. For W/O Points, it was the second time he lost his leader that day. Harold Knight was a South African from Cape Province, and had been with the squadron for just three weeks.

Note on the aircraft: TOC No.20 MU 23.12.43, issued to No.137 Sqn at a unrecorded date. Served previously with No.1 Sqn.

23.05.44   S/L Jack **BRANDT**   RAF No.39349   RAF   **MN474**   SF-E   IB   **Eva.**

Took off at 1555, S/L Brandt leading four aircraft on a RANGER operation covering the route Amiens-Montdidier-Laon-St-Quentin and Cambrai-Aire and Cassel. Flying along at deck-level, a goods train was observed, two miles east of Aire, and four attacks made. Strikes were observed and clouds of steam and smoke were seen coming from the loco. There was light flak from the centre of the train, and considerable heavy flak from a nearby airstrip. S/L Brandt was last seen making a circuit at 200', after which a heavy explosion followed. The rest of the formation, under F/L Brandreth, landed at base at 18.15. Posted in as supernumerary Squadron Leader in March, Brandt served in Far East with No.67 Sqn, flying Buffaloes between March 1941 and June 1942, becoming its CO in January. One confirmed victory, No.67 Sqn, Burma, 1941. DFC [No.67 Sqn].

Note on the aircraft: TOC No.51 MU 11.04.44, issued to No.137 Sqn 18.05.44.

25.05.44 W/O Albert **Witham**   RAF No.1336599   RAF   **MN469**   SF-K   IB   †

Six Typhoons (4 RPs and 2 Fighters) took off at 09.00 and flew at deck level to a point approximately 1 mile outside the entrance to Ostende Harbour. Here a 600 ton coaster was found lying stationary facing eastwards. W/O Albert Witham led the rocket attack and of the four salvoes, two made direct hits at the water line, one at the bow and the other on the stern. The stern superstructure disintegrated and large volumes of dense black smoke and flames were observed. The vessel was sinking at the bows and listing heavily to port. There was intense light flak from the shore, and M/G fire from a small trawler that was lying some 300 yards to the west. This and the sinking vessel were then raked with cannon, during the course of which Witham was hit by flak and seen to go down in flames at around 09.20. Pilot had served in the squadron for over 15 months and was close to finishing his tour.

Note on the aircraft: TOC No.51 MU 11.04.44, issued to No.137 Sqn 18.05.44.

06.07.44 W/O Alfred W. **Emslie**   Aus.414130   RAAF   **MN468**   SF-G   IB   -

Returning from an early morning anti-diver patrol, the constant speed unit failed causing over speeding. Emslie carried out a successful forced landing wheels up and was unhurt. The aircraft caught fire and was totally destroyed. Alfred Emslie was an Australian from Queensland and had joined the squadron in May 1943. (see also operational losses 09.07.44 and accident losses 29.04.44).

Note on the aircraft: TOC No.20 MU 04.04.44, issued to No.137 Sqn 19.04.44.

09.07.44 W/O Alfred W. **Emslie**   Aus.414130   RAAF   **MN556**   SF-E   IB   **Inj.**

Took off at 01.30 for an early morning anti-diver patrol. The sortie was uneventful but on landing his aircraft bounced and commenced to swing. Emlsie corrected but the Typhoon came off the runway and nose turned over. He was taken to hospital seriously wounded on the right eye, and eventually did not returned to the squadron, being later declared permanently medically unfit for aircrew duties. (see also operational losses 06.07.44 and accident losses 29.04.44).

Note on the aircraft: TOC No.20 MU 04.04.44, issued to No.137 Sqn 11.05.44.

27.07.44 F/O Ralph A. **Johnstone**   Can./J.22310   RCAF   **MN156**   SF-V   IB   †

Took off at 08.20 for an anti-diver patrol. Collided in cloud with his No.2 and was seen obviously out of control before crashing near Denton Court at 08.38. A Canadian, native of Saskatchewan, it was his first tour of operations. He had been made Temporary A Flight commander since H.C. Knight's death on 21.05.44, and had served with the squadron for a year.

Note on the aircraft: TOC date unrecorded, issued to No.137 Sqn date unrecorded but aircraft probably coming from No.56 Sqn.

   F/Sgt Arthur R. **Hack**   RAF No.1388930   RAF   **MN596**   SF-Q   IB   †

See above. Arthur Hack had only just joined the squadron earlier in the month..

Note on the aircraft: TOC No.51 MU 15.04.44, issued to No.137 Sqn 18.05.44.

04.08.44 F/O James C. **Holder**   Can./J.25779   RCAF   **JR511**   IB   †

Four Typhoons (2 fighters and two RPs) took off at 16.05 for an armed recce to Colijnsplaat, and also to investigate a 2,000-ton vessel attacked earlier in the day. Two coasters of 400/500 tons and 1 small M/V were found stationary just off shore, west of Colijnsplaat, and attacked. P/O Nicholls undershot with RP salvo, and F/O Holder scored a near miss with his, while P/Os Ashworth and Gates observed cannon strikes on both coasters. F/O Holder turned and went in for second attack, but crashed in the sea between the ships and the coast, apparently having been hit by flak. The others returned at 17.15, Nicholls' aircraft having been hit by flak and debris (JP663). Posted to the squadron in May James Holder was Canadian, and a native of Ontario. Commissioned in April 1943 he had embarked for the UK the following August.

Note on the aircraft: TOC No.20 MU 01.01.44. Issued to No.137 Sqn 17.07.44. Previously served with No.198 Sqn.

18.08.44 F/L Matthew **Wood**   Can./J.5540   RCAF   **MN126**   SF-X   IB   †

Four Typhoons were detailed at 17.15 to complete an armed recce of Vimoutiers area, F/L Brandreth leading. Attacks on transports were made, 12 being claimed as damaged. F/L Wood was shot down by flak in the process, his aircraft exploding on the ground while W/O Shemeld (No.4) was also badly shot up (EK289). Aircraft returned to base at 18.00. A Canadian from British Columbia, pilot had been a Flying Instructor in Canada before arriving in the UK during August 1943. He had been with the squadron since May.

Note on the aircraft: TOC No.51 MU 02.01.44. Issued to No.137 Sqn date unrecorded. Previously served with No.56 Sqn.

27.08.44   F/O Ian C. **HUTCHESON**   NZ412694   RNZAF   **MN803**   SF-V   IB   †

Seven Typhoons took off at 12.15, under F/L Brandreth, their brief to attack shipping between Le Havre and Rouen (France). motor boats were seen crossing the Seine and were attacked with R.P.s and all destroyed. Six barges, and 8 METs, were also destroyed, the latter left burning on the wharf. During the attack F/O Ian Hutcheson (No.3) was hit by flak, and he radioed that he was about to bale out. No parachute was seen and it is believed that he died in his plane when it crashed. Returning pilots landed at 13.05. Hutcheson was a New Zealander who had joined the squadron during June. He'd previously completed a tour of operations with No.3 Sqn between May 1942 and April 1943.

Note on the aircraft: TOC No.5 MU 04.06.44. Issued to No.137 Sqn date unrecorded. Previously served with No.198 Sqn.

20.09.44   Sgt Alexander H.O. **BUTLER**   RAF No.1806512   RAF   **PD551**   SF-U   IB   †

8 RP Typhoons took off at 13.53, led by the CO, Major Piltingsrud, detailed to attack tanks north of the River Neder Rijn, in the Arnhem area. No movement was seen and owing to the weather, which was 10/10 cloud and haze on the deck, no attacks were carried out. The aircraft of Sgt Butler was seen to burst into flames and crashed on the way home, all the others landing back at base at 14.46. Alexander Butler was raised in India, where his father was a regular Indian Army Officer. He had received his commission on 13th August, but was still wearing his Sergeant stripes when he was killed.

Note on the aircraft: TOC No.51 MU 30.08.44. Issued to No.137 Sqn from No.83 GSU where it was last recorded on 07.09.44.

23.09.44   W/O Thomas J. **PIKE**   RAF No.1316008   RAF   **MN421**   SF-D   IB   -

For the last mission of the day, four RP Typhoons led by F/L W.B. Short and 8 RP Tphoons of No.182 Sqn were detailed to attack mortars and infantry targets, taking off at 18.35. On return by 20.00, they had to land on the dark and on landing Pike's aircraft ran into an aircraft of No.182 Sqn. Pilot escaped injuries, but the aircraft was declared Cat.E. Not much is known on this pilot except that he had joined the squadron during the summer.

Note on the aircraft: TOC No.51 MU, issued to No.137 Sqn date unrecorded. Served previously with Nos.245 & 247 Sqns until 17.06.44 when it was damaged in a flying accident.

24.09.44   S/L Gunnar **PILTINGSRUD**   N.1084   RNAF   **MN955**   SF-G   IB   †

Led by the CO, 8 RP Typhoons were detailed at 16.01 to attacks trains East of Goth (Germany). Three were attacked with rockets, and all were damaged. Soon afterwards 30 FW190s appeared and engaged and the CO was shot down in the ensuing combat. The rest of the formation landed safely at 16.48. Gunnar Piltinsgrud, a former officer in the Norwegian Merchant Fleet, was abroad when Norway was invaded and joined the RAF during the summer of 1940. After training as a pilot he sent to No.331 (Norwegian) Sqn in September 1941. He stayed a short time with this unit and was posted to No.258 and No.615 Squadrons before joining No.332 (Norwegian) Sqn in January 1942. In June he left for No.56 Sqn, flying the troublesome Typhoon, and remained with this unit until his tour ended in July 1943. He was awarded the DFC and returned to operational duty in January 1944, rejoining No.56 Sqn before his posting to No.137 Sqn in March 1944. When he was shot down, he was completing his 52nd sortie with the squadron.

Note on the aircraft: TOC No.5 MU 29.06.44. Issued to No.137 Sqn 17.07.44.

28.09.44   F/O David W. **GUTTRIDGE**   RAF No.150045   RAF   **MP125**   SF-M   IB   †

8 RP Typhoons led by S/L Brough were detailed to carry out an Armed Recce of the area Emmerich-Cleve-Kranenberg-Afferden-Goch. No movement was seen on road or rail but intense and accurate light flak was encountered near Kassel. Guttridge was hit and as no word was heard from him, it is believed that he had been killed instantly. 'Gutts' Guttridge had been with the squadron since January.

Note on the aircraft: TOC No.51 MU 15.07.44. Issued to No.137 Sqn 20.08.44.

            P/O Henry T. **NICHOLLS**   RAF No.174073   RAF   **MN169**   SF-J   IB   **PoW**

As above. Baled out and was last seen drifting north. Henry Nichols had been a member of the squadron for 3 months.

Note on the aircraft: TOC 23.01.44. Issued to No.137 Sqn 30.04.44 from No.56 Sqn.

30.09.44   F/Sgt Mark J. **WHITBY**   AUS.413056   RAAF   **MN627**   SF-N   IB   -

Took off at 12.21 with 7 others RP Typhoons, led by F/L Short, to attack a village that had been 'marked' with red smoke. Following the attack Whitby crash-landed behind Allied lines, and was picked by the Army, with slight head injuries. The remaining aircraft landed back at base at 13.07. A native of New South Wales, Whitby had been with the squadron since May, and was commissioned during October. He completed his tour in April 1945.

Note on the aircraft: TOC No.5 MU 02.05.44. Issued to No.137 Sqn 26.05.44.

11.10.44   F/O Russel S. **WILSON**   CAN./J.25388   RCAF   **JP663**   SF-B   IB   **PoW**

At 13.48 seven RPs Typhoons, led by S/L Brough, took off to carry out an Armed Recce. After a couple of minutes of flight a suspected wood containing enemy targets was attacked. F/O Wilson (Red 2) was hit by intense light flak, and his aircraft caught fire, forcing him to land behind enemy lines. A Canadian, native of Ontario, he sailed to the UK in May 1943 and had only joined the squadron a couple of days previously. Wilson was later reported PoW at Stalag Luft III.

Note on the aircraft: TOC No.51 MU 30.08.43. Issued to No.137 Sqn 17.07.44. Previously served with No.183 Sqn.

29.10.44   P/O Edwin **ASHWORTH**   RAF No.177903   RAF   **MN995**   SF-X   IB   -

Six RP Typhoons took off at 10.45, with F/O Gates (RAAF) leading, to carry out an Armed Recce in the Venlo-Roermond and bomb line area. Four barges were attacked and damaged and a flak post was destroyed at about 10 miles SW of Venlo. During the attack light and heavy flak was encountered and P/O Ashworth was shot down at 1130. Pilot was able to bale out over Allied lines. Edwin Ashworth had joined the squadron in August 1943, and successfully completed his tour in January 1945.

Note on the aircraft: TOC No.5 MU 15.07.44. Issued to No.137 Sqn 20.08.44.

18.11.44   F/O Noel J.M. **MANFRED**   AUS.413627   RAAF   **MN191**   SF-P   IB   †

6 RP Typhoons, led by F/L Tickner, took off at 11.20 to carry out an Armed Recce of the Sittard-Erkelenez-Heinsberg area. When airborne section was instructed to attack enemy troops concentrated in Randeram village, which they did with cannon and three salvoes of rockets. Intensive accurate light flak was experienced from the target and F/O Manfred was hit and shot down, five aircraft returning at base at 12.05. Noel Manfred was a native of New South Wales, Australia and had served with the squadron since May. He previously had flown with No.1683 BDT Flight.

Note on the aircraft: TOC 23.01.44. Issued to No.137 Sqn 30.04.44 from No.56 Sqn.

19.11.44   F/O Michael J.B. **COLE**   RAF No.156033   RAF   **JR207**   SF-B   IB   -

7 RP Typhoons took off at 15.11, under W/C North Lewis DFC, together with 8 Typhoons of 247 Sqn. Formation was detailed to attack enemy movement in the village of Wurm, the second time that day this target was attacked. F/O Cole did not reform after attack and was forced to land 1/4 mile east of Shepenrsal, where he was picked up by American Forces slightly injured. He returned to the squadron at 20.15 that night. The rest of the formation landed back at base at 15.55. Michael Cole had served with the unit since June 1944 and was posted away in February 1945.

Note on the aircraft: TOC No.51 MU 19.10.43. Issued to No.137 Sqn 18.09.44. Served also with No.400 (RCAF) Sqn on non operational trials.

05.12.44   F/O John **GATES**   AUS.409401   RAAF   **MN586**   SF-G   IB   **PoW**

F/O Gates took off at 11.04 to lead 6 RPs Typhoons detailed to carry out an Armed Recce of the area Wessel-Munster-Bocholt. A loco and 12 trucks moving East were attacked and damaged, and a factory north of Dinslaken also damaged with rockets and cannon. Considerable heavy and light flak was experienced from Dinslaken and Gate's aircraft shot down, the pilot baling out North of the town. All other aircraft returned safely to base at 12.18. John Gates was a native of New South Wales, Australia and had served in the squadron since May 1943.

Note on the aircraft: TOC No.51 MU 11.04.44. Issued to No.137 Sqn 18.05.44.

26.12.44   W/O William A. **FLETT**   CAN./R.124871   RCAF   **JP504**   SF-E   IB   †

Six RP Typhoons took off at 09.50, led by P/O Colton. Their brief was to carry out an Armed Recce in the area of Hauffalize-Bulange-St-Vith. Scattered MET moving west and 6 armoured cars, were attacked and strikes seen on one vehicle. W/O Flett was thought to have been hit by flak and his aircraft seen to crash from 200 feet. The remaining pilots returned to base, landing at 10.54. A Canadian, native of Nova Scotia, Flett was commissioned as J.98897 but was still awaiting official notification.

Note on the aircraft: TOC date unrecorded. Issued to No.137 Sqn 22.08.44 as SF-R. Ken Brain's aircraft until recoded SF-E in November 1944. Served also with No.197 Sqn.

27.12.44   P/O Norman F. **SWIFT**   AUS.411404   RAAF   **MN234**   SF-T   IB   **PoW**

Six RP Typhoons took off at 12.08, led by F/L Tickner, being ordered to carry out an Armed Recce in the Houffalize-Bullange-Clervauz base area. No targets were sighted but intense light flak was encountered South and East of St-Vith, hitting P/O Swift. He was last seen diving down, about 10 miles East of St-Vith, but did not give any indication of the nature of his trouble or what he was planning to do. The reminder of the patrol landed at 13.32 at base. Swift was a native of New South Wales, Australia, and had earlier flown with No.453 (RAAF) Sqn between July 1942 and March 1943. He had then been on sick leave, for almost a year, until January 1944, and joined No.137 Sqn during September.

Note on the aircraft: TOC No.20 MU 04.02.44. Issued to No.137 Sqn 21.09.44. served also with No.198 Sqn.

29.12.44   F/L John L. **CROSSLEY**   RAF No.100647   RAF   **RB194**   IB   **PoW**
8 RP Typhoons took off at 11.21, led by F/L Crossley, to carry out a long-range Armed Recce in the Meppen, and SW of Bremen, areas. Attacked four trains moving south claiming the four locomotives as destroyed. Crossley was hit by flak and force to land. Remainder of patrol strafed a radio station and later 2 locos pushing and pulling 15 trucks near Choppenburg, destroying the two locos and returning to base at 13.21. Crossley had previously served in No.247 Sqn and had only arrived at the squadron a few days before.
Note on the aircraft: TOC No.51 MU 20.09.44. Issued to No.137 Sqn 17.10.44.

31.12.44   P/O James A.D. **SHEMELD**   RAF No.185729   RAF   **MN660**   SF-K   IB   †
8 RP Typhoons, fitted with long range tanks, took off at 13.35, led by P/O Shemeld for an Armed Recce in the Mappen-Shedinghausen-Menhaus area. A stationary train facing south was located and attacked, and the loco destroyed. Another train moving south was attacked during which P/O Shemeld was shot down in flames by light flak. He was the longest serving member of the squadron, at that time, and had been with it for 18 months. The remaining aircraft returned to base at 15.45.
Note on the aircraft: TOC No.5 MU 02.05.44. Issued to No.137 Sqn 27.05.44.

01.01.45   F/Sgt Laurence A.V. **BURROWS**   RAF No.958745   RAF   **JR261**   SF-Z   IB   †
Killed while taxiing towards dispersal during Bodenplatte operation. Arrived at the squadron in January 1944 and, although recently commissioned as 188890, was still wearing his NCO stripes.
Note on the aircraft: TOC No.51 MU 06.11.43. Issued to No.137 Sqn 26.11.44. Also with Nos.174 & 182 Sqns.

03.02.45   F/Sgt Albert V. **CRORY**   RAF No.1576679   RAF   **RB252**   SF-T   IB   †
Six aircraft took off at 13.16, for an Armed Recce in the Munster area, F/L Rendall leading. The formation flew at 5,000 ft and when arriving over the area they attacked MET, which had been reported moving east from the town. The targets were found to be in a well-spaced line and did not appear to be a military movement. Two attacks were made with unobserved results, owing to a great deal of smoke in the same area. Intense light and heavy flak was experienced and F/Sgt 'Paddy' Crory was hit and shot down. In all, half of the participating aircraft received hits although they all returned safely, landing at 14.33. 'Paddy' Crory had served with the squadron since May 1944.
Note on the aircraft: TOC No.20 MU 05.10.44. Issued to No.137 Sqn 10.11.44.

24.03.45   F/O Richard A. **EGLEY**   NZ421690   RNZAF   **RB376**   SF-C   IB   †
8 Typhoons, led by F/L Rendall, carried out an anti-flak patrol, taking off at 10.02. F/O Egley was leading the second section of four aircraft. Four guns, and then a light flak position, were attacked but Egley's aircraft was hit. He was seen to bale out South of Brünen, and to land safely, but was later found dead near the scene of the crash. 'Dick' Egley was a New Zealander and had served in the squadron since May 1944. The remaining aircraft returned at 10.47.
Note on the aircraft: TOC No.51 MU 10.11.44. Issued to No.137 Sqn 22.03.45 from No.168 Sqn.

26.03.45   P/O John W.C. **COLLINS**   Aus.4521571   RAAF   **JP736**   IB   -
P/O Collins took off at 18.29 as part of a patrol, led by S/L Barraclough, on an Armed Recce over Brünen. It was the last planned sortie of the day and lasted one hour. Three lorries were attacked and silenced, and a tank was destroyed later, followed by an attack on 6 MET, two of which were destroyed. 'Will' Collins was hit by flak and crash-landed near the autobahn. He was a native of New South Wales (Australia), and had served with the squadron from January 1945, until being repatriated in July.
Note on the aircraft: TOC No.20 MU 31.08.43. Served with Nos.175, 182 and 247 Sqns before to be issued to No.137 Sqn in March 1945 (precise date unrecorded).

F/Sgt John A.H.G. **PENNANT**   RAF No.1387662   RAF   **RB454**   IB   -
As above. Baled out over Allied lines and was seen to wave. 'Johnny' Pennant had been with the squadron since October 1944
Note on the aircraft: TOC No.5 MU 08.12.44. Issued to No.137 Sqn date unrecorded probably the same day it was issued to No.83 GSU (20.02.45).

01.04.45   Sgt Patrick A. **LANGLEY**   RAF No.1804392   RAF   **EK128**   IB   -
6 Typhoons, led by F/L JM Key, took off at 09.28 for an Armed Recce over Osnabruck-Lingen-Rheine area. Despite poor weather and cloud base being at 1,000 ft, attacks were made on MET in the Lingen area, and 5 claimed as damaged. Sgt Langley was hit

by flak and came down near the aerodrome of Rheine. His No.1, F/L Adams, saw the aircraft on fire but Langley escaped and hid in a barn for 3 days until British troops arrived in the area. The remaining aircraft returned at base at 10.51. Langley had joined the squadron the previous month and was to remain with it until disbandment.

Note on the aircraft: TOC No.20 MU 28.02.43. Issued to No.137 Sqn 01.10.44. Also with No.174 Sqn.

	Sgt Frederick A. **EDWARDS**	RAF No.1604041	RAF	**RB193**	SF-U	IB	†

As above. Sgt Edwards force-landed to the East of Munster. His No.1 (P/O Forrest) did not see him landing, but Edwards said over the RT that he thought he could get down safely, but he was killed. He had only joined the squadron the previous month.

Note on the aircraft: TOC No.51 MU 20.09.44. Issued to No.137 Sqn 01.03.45. Also with No.182 Sqn.

04.04.45	F/O John R. **NIXON**	CAN./J.26410	RCAF	**MN863**	SF-S	IB	**Inj.**

6 Typhoons took off at 15.58, led by F/L Key, for an Armed Recce over Linden-Meppen-Cloppenburg area. An attack was made on 4 towed guns that were seen in the Liden area, two being destroyed and two damaged. Two MET were also destroyed and three damaged in the same area. Light flak was experienced and F/O J.R. Nixon was apparently hit. He made a force landing half a mile South of Wardhausen, but unfortunately the aircraft turned on to its back and broke up. Nixon was pulled out by some Army soldiers and found to have nothing more than a broken right arm. The other aircraft were reported back at base at 17.35. 'Hank' Nixon was a Canadian, a native of Ontario, who sailed for the UK in June 1943 and had served with No.401 (RCAF) Sqn between August and November 1943. He was repatriated to Canada in June 1945.

Note on the aircraft: TOC No.51 MU 02.06.44. Issued to No.137 Sqn 01.02.45. Also with No.245 Sqn.

12.04.45	W/O Robert S. **KNIGHT-CLARKE**	RAF No.1382060	RAF	**JR444**		IB	†

8 Typhoons, let by Capt Watt (SAAF), took off at 08.02 for an Armed Recce over Oldenberg-Zeven-Rotherburg-Rethen area. A loco and 2 trucks were damaged, and 2 MET destroyed. Four barges were also attacked and damaged with cannon. W/O Knight-Clarke's aircraft was hit by flak and crashed in flames near Kampe. He had arrived at the squadron during March.

Note on the aircraft: TOC No.51 MU 02.12.43. Issued to No.137 Sqn 05.04.45. Also with No.439 (RCAF), 168 Sqn.

14.04.45	F/Sgt John A.H.G. **PENNANT**	RAF No.1387662	RAF	**MP154**		IB	†

Took off at 17.01, with 3 other Typhoons, to attack houses near Verden. A factory amongst the houses was hit and damaged, and Pennant's aircraft was struck by light flak and crashed, exploding on the ground. The mission lasted less than an hour.

Note on the aircraft: TOC No.5 MU 28.07.44. Issued to No.137 Sqn 05.04.45.

OTHER TYPE
(HURRICANE)

01.01.45	-	-	-	**V7752**	SF-?	I	-

Destroyed in air raid, Eindhoven (Netherlands). This Hurricane was issued to the squadron as communication aircraft on 20 January 1944 and received a question mark as individual marking. It later received full D-Day markings and met its final fate on 1 January 1945 when it was destroyed on the ground during Operation 'Bodenplatte'.

Note on the aircraft: TOC 07.12.40. Served with No.96 Sqn then with various second line units or as communication aircraft with No.263 Sqn. It was issued to No.137 Sqn on 20.01.44 for the same purpose.

Total: 67

APPENDIX VI
AIRCRAFT LOST BY ACCIDENT

WHIRLWIND

28.10.41   S/L John **SAMPLE**   AAF No.90378   RAF   **P7053**   I   †
Collided with another Whirlwind, during formation practice, and lost part of the tail, crashing near Englishcombe. John Sample was a pre-war Auxiliary Air Force officer, serving in No.607 Sqn at the outbreak of war and then in France. During the Battle of France he took command of No.504 Sqn, leading it until the end of his tour in March 1941. His second tour of operations saw him appointed as the first commanding officer of No.137 Sqn, although his accident occurred just a month later. Three confirmed victories, including two shared with No.607 Sqn, Battle of France and No.504 Sqn, Battle of Britain. DFC [No.504 sqn].
Note on the aircraft:TOC No.18 MU 12.06.41, issued No.137 Sqn 28.09.41.

09.03.42   P/O Charles W. **DE-SHANE**   CAN./J.15148   RCAF   **P7036**   I   †
Spun off a turn, during dogfight with a Spitfire, and crashed on White Horse Common, North Walsham, Norfolk. Charles De-Shane was a Canadian from Ontario, posted in from No.56 OTU in November 1941. He trained in Canada and had sailed for the UK in September that same year.
Note on the aircraft:TOC No.39 MU 22.04.41, issued No.137 Sqn 28.09.41.

04.05.42   P/O Robert E.D. **WRIGHT**   CAN./J.15147   RCAF   **P7103**   I   †
Lost a wing during aerobatics one mile N of Aylsham, Norfolk. Robert Wright was a Canadian from Ontario, posted to the squadron for his first tour of operations in January 1942.
Note on the aircraft:TOC No.18 MU 18.08.41, issued No.137 Sqn 27.11.41.

30.06.42   -   **P7101**   SF-A   I   -
Hit while parked at Matlask, by Lysander N1249, and declared damaged beyond repair.
Note on the aircraft:TOC No.18 MU 07.08.41, issued No.137 Sqn 18.04.42.

13.01.43   Sgt Edmund A. **BOLSTER**   RAF No.1090706   RAF   **P7061**   I   -
Collided with P7102 while taxying on wet grass, Manston. 'Paddy' Bolster arrived at the squadron for his first operational posting in October 1942. In June 1943, he was posted to No.247 Sqn, with which he flew until the end of his tour in August 1944. He was never commissioned.
Note on the aircraft:TOC No.39 MU 27.05.41, issued No.137 Sqn 07.11.42. Saw first action with No.263 Sqn between September and December 1941.

30.03.43   P/O John T. **DAVIDSON**   RAF No.114577   RAF   **P7104**   I   -
Engine cut in flight and landed on bad ground at Manston, collapsing undercarriage. 'Paddy' Davidson was a newcomer to the squadron and was later killed in action (see entry 14.08.43).
Note on the aircraft:TOC No.18 MU 30.08.41, issued No.137 Sqn 14.04.42. FH: 319.0

15.04.43   P/O John M. **HADOW**   RAF No.122121   RAF   **P7121**   SF-C   I   †
Hit ground during dive-bombing practice. John Hadow was a newcomer, who had been commissioned in March 1942. His previous postings are not known.
Note on the aircraft:TOC No.39 MU 08.12.41, issued No.137 Sqn 06.02.42. FH: 325.6.

01.05.43   Sgt Aubrey C. **SMITH**   RAF No.1340628   RAF   **P6976**   I   -
Wing hit ground on landing at Manston. Aubrey Smith joined the squadron in November 1942, completing his tour in January 1944, when he was commissioned. He was awarded the DFM in September 1943, not only the sole member of the squadron to receive this decoration, but also the only one awarded to a Whirlwind pilot.
Note on the aircraft:TOC direct to No.263 Sqn on 07.11.40. Issued to No.137 Sqn 20.02.42.

HURRICANE

31.07.43   Sgt John McG. **BARCLAY**   RAF No.655794   RAF   **KZ657**   IV   †
Stalled while flying at low level, during a practice air combat, and crashed at Maldon, Essex. 'Tich' Barclay had been posted in from No.263 Sqn during February 1943, with whom he served for four months.
Note on the aircraft: TOC No.44 MU 21.04.43. Issued to No.137 Sqn 21.06.43. FH: 24.1

TYPHOON

25.03.44   F/O David W. **GUTTRIDGE**   RAF No.150045   RAF   **MM972**   SF-F   IB   -
Engine cut in navex and bellylanded near Dymchurch (St.Marys in the Marsh). 'Gutts' Guttridge had joined the squadron two months before and was later killed in action (see entry 28.09.44).
Note on the aircraft: TOC No.20 MU 21.12.43, issued to No.137 Sqn 18.01.44.

25.04.44   F/O David T.N. **KELLY**   RAF No.124453   RAF   **MN117**   SF-B   IB   -
While taking off from Manston for a training flight, hit a bulldozer. David Kelly had just joined the squadron. In June 1944 he was posted to AFU, later serving with No.174 Sqn as CO between January and March 1945.
Note on the aircraft: TOC No.51 MU 02.01.44 issued No.137 Sqn unrecorded. Previously issued to No.56 Sqn for a short time.

29.04.44   W/O Alfred W. **EMSLIE**   Aus.414130   RAAF   **MN180**   SF-Q   IB   -
Engine cut in circuit due to fuel shortage and forcelanded at Ruan Manor, near Predannack, Cornwall. Alfred Emslie was an Australian from Queensland and had joined the squadron in May 1943. He was later seriously wounded in action on 09.07.44 (see also operational losses 06.07.44).
Note on the aircraft: TOC No.51 MU 14.01.44, issued No.137 Sqn unrecorded. Previously issued to No.56 Sqn for a short time.

21.11.44   F/O John R. **BALDWIN**   Can./J.25777   RCAF   **MN533**   SF-E   IB   -
Burst a tyre on take-off and had to belly land at B.78 on his return from a training flight. John Russell, a Canadian living in Ontario, not John Robert, another Typhoon pilot, English, DSO, DFC & BAR who commanded a Typhoon wing, No.123 by the end of war. Commissioned in April 1943, John Russell served at first in Canada with No.130 Squadron, RCAF between May 1943 and March 1944, then sailed for the UK arriving in May. No details available between May and October 1944. Repatriated to Canada in July 1945.
Note on the aircraft: TOC No.5 MU 12.04.44, issued to No.137 Sqn 21.09.44.

05.12.44   W/O William A. **FLETT**   Can./R.124871   RCAF   **PD609**   IB   -
Crash-landed while ferrying the Typhoon to No.137 Sqn. A Canadian, native of Nova Scotia. Posted to the squadron for his first tour of operations that same month, he was killed in action two weeks later. (See entry 26.12.44)
Note on the aircraft: TOC No.51 MU 20.09.44, issued to No.137 Sqn from No.83 GSU the date of the crash.

23.06.45   F/Sgt James H. **NUTTER**   RAF No.1450367   RAF   **SW426**   SF-V   IB   †
Dived into the sea 400-500 metres from Keldsnoi lighthouse, SW of Langaland, on flight back to Husum from Vaerlose (satellite of B.160 -Copenhagen). The Navy tried to locate the body, albeit without success. James Nutter had arrived at the squadron in April for his first operational posting.
Note on the aircraft:TOC No.5 MU 28.01.45. Issued to No.137 Sqn 22.03.45.

30.06.45   S/L Douglas **MURRAY**   RAF No.119128   RAF   **SW561**   SF-M   IB   -
While orbiting, prior to landing at Varerlose near Kobenhvn, S/L Murray saw his engine cut and was forced to make a wheels-up landing. Aircraft was categorised Cat.B, but subsequently not repaired. 'Slug' Murray, a former Army officer, volunteered to trans-fer to the RAF to become a pilot and by mid-1942, he was serving with No.26 Sqn, an Army co-operations unit, with which he was awarded a DFC in March 1943. He completed his tour in January 1944. For his second tour of operations, he converted onto

Typhoons, and was posted to No.181 Sqn in September 1944, then No.182 Sqn, in December, as a Flight Commander, before joining No.137 Sqn, in March 1945, as CO. He died in 1947 in a motor accident. 'Slug' was coming from 'Slugger' due his process as a boxer in the Army.

<u>Note on the aircraft</u>:TOC No.51 MU 17.03.45. Issued to No.137 Sqn 05.04.45.

01.08.45	P/O Jack A. **CUNNINGHAM**	RAF No.197815	RAF	**MM966**	IB	-

At 10.50, while taking off for a practice formation flight, P/O Jack Cunningham had the port tyre burst, obliging him to make a belly landing at Lubeck (B.158) at the return of the flight. Aircraft declared Cat.E. Pilot had served in the squadron since February 1945.

<u>Note on the aircraft</u>: TOC No.51 MU 22.12.43. Served two times with No.137 Sqn, between 04.01.44 and 24.04.44 and in 1945 but the date is not recorded. In the meantime it also served with Nos.175 and 184 Sqns.

11.08.45	F/L Chistopher **PEIRSON-JONES**	RAF No.162846	RAF	**SW510**	IB	-

While practising aerobatics and formation flying, suffered an engine failure at about 8,000 feet, the result of a serious oil leak. The engine then picked up, operating normally until aircraft descended to 1,000 feet, when the it seized necessitating pilot to make a forced landing, 1 mile NW of the village of Havighorst. The pilot, who had operated with the squadron since April, was uninjured.

<u>Note on the aircraft</u>: TOC No.5 MU 16.03.45, issued to No.137 Sqn 05.05.45.

MAGISTER

13.04.43	W/C Guy P. **GIBSON**	RAF No.39438	RAF	**T9908**	I	-

W/C Gibson took off for an airfield recce when the engine of the Magister failed. In attempting to make a force landing, the aircraft hit anti-glider obstructions and crashed near Birchington, Kent. Gibson, prior to becoming famous with the Barnes Wallis 'bouncing bombs' and Dambuster raid, had begun his career pre-war as a bomber pilot with No.83 Sqn, flying Hampdens. During the autumn of 1940 he underwent night fighter training and joined No.29 Sqn, with which he claimed 3 confirmed victories and received the DFC & BAR. He returned to Bomber Command in 1942 to lead No.106 Sqn and was awarded the DSO. When he borro -wed the squadron's Magister he was about to prepare for the famous raid, with the Wallis bombs, at the head of the newly-formed No.617 Sqn. He won the VC for the raid, which took place in May 1943. Although officially off operations he completed a sortie on the night of 19/20 September 1944, but his Mosquito XX KB267 crashed on the return journey, killing himself and his navigator.

<u>Note on the aircraft</u>: TOC No.48 MU 26.09.40, issued to No.137 Sqn 02.11.41.

Total: 19
including 18 combat aircraft

APPENDIX VII
Aircraft serial numbers matching
with
individual letters

SF-A
P6993, P7061, P7093, P7101 (*Whirlwind*)
KZ608 (*Hurricane*)
JR497, MN455 (*Typhoon*)

SF-B
KZ661 (*Hurricane*)
JP663, JR207, JR535, MN117, MN145,
MN429, MN822, RB254, SW473
(*Typhoon*)

SF-C
P7121 (*Whirlwind*)
KW918, KX829 (*Hurricane*)
MM969, MN117, MN586, MN980, MP125,
RB376, SW402 (*Typhoon*)

SF-D
P7106 (*Whirlwind*)
KZ710 (*Hurricane*)
JR247, MM966, MN351, MN421, MN455
(*Typhoon*)

SF-E
KX698, KZ655 (*Hurricane*)
JP504, JR532, MN474, MN533, MN556
(*Typhoon*)

SF-F
KZ698, KZ576 (*Hurricane*)
MM972, MN306, MN556 (*Typhoon*)

SF-G
P7058 (*Whirlwind*)
KZ676 (*Hurricane*)
JR327, MM969, MM978, MN468, MN586,

MN955, PD570 (*Typhoon*)

SF-H
P7005, P7095 (*Whirlwind*)
KX827 (*Hurricane*)
EK270, JR516, MN575 (*Typhoon*)

SF-I

SF-J
KX585 (*Hurricane*)
JR247, MN169, MN312 (*Typhoon*)

SF-K
KZ399 (*Hurricane*)
MN469, MN660 (*Typhoon*)

SF-L
JR504, MN198 (*Typhoon*)

SF-M
EK289, MN289, MN531, MP125, SW461
(*Typhoon*)

SF-N
MN134, MN627 (*Typhoon*)

SF-O

SF-P
P7098, P7102 (*Whirlwind*)
MN191, MN922 (*Typhoon*)

SF-Q
JR500, MN180, MN596, RB252
(*Typhoon*)

SF-R
JP504, MM974, MN460, PD611 (*Typhoon*)

SF-S
P6982, P7055 (*Whirlwind*)
KZ660 (*Hurricane*)
MN134, MN863 (*Typhoon*)

SF-T
JR433, MN152, MN234, MP133, RB252,
RB318 (*Typhoon*)

SF-U
P7011, P7055 (*Whirlwind*)
MN584, PD536, PD551, RB193 (*Typhoon*)

SF-V
P7012 (*Whirlwind*)
MN156, MN262, MN803, RB504, SW426
(*Typhoon*)

SF-W
P7002, P7119 (*Whirlwind*)
DN492, MM980, JR437, MM980, MN584,
MN632 (*Typhoon*)

SF-X
KW918, KZ520 (*Hurricane*)
JR530, MN126, MN374, MN995
(*Typhoon*)

SF-Y
JR305 (*Typhoon*)

SF-Z
JP583, JR261, JR505, MM990, MN357,
MN792 (*Typhoon*)

SF-?
V7752 (*Hurricane*)

RAAF

J.W. **CARTER**, Aus.412912
J.W.C. **COLLINS**, Aus.421571
H.A. **COPEMAN**, Aus.425607
A.W. **EMSLIE**, Aus.414130
J.T.N. **FROST**, Aus.412514
J. **GATES**, Aus.409401
L.J. **HODGE**, Aus.430450
J.A. **HORNE**, Aus.405973
E.L. **JAMES**, Aus.422566
N.J.M. **MANFRED**, Aus.413627
E.L. **MUSGRAVE**, Aus.403528
C. **NEAL**, Aus.413236
J. **RENDALL**, Aus.413663
G.C. **SHELDON**, Aus.420282
N.F. **SWIFT**, Aus.411404
H.G. **TURNER**, Aus.409620, *NEW ZEALAND*
M.J. **WHITBY**, Aus.413056
R. **WRIGHT**, Aus.411978

RAF

A.V. **ALBERTINI**, RAF No.800544
J.W. **ALLEN**, RAF No.135866
J.R. **ALLWOOD**, RAF No.1607898
W.M. **ANDREWS**, RAF No.?
E. **ASHWORTH**, RAF No.177903
J.McG. **BARCLAY**, RAF No.655794
E.K. **BARNES**, RAF No.44135
R.G.V. **BARRACLOUGH**, RAF No.66487
L.H. **BARTLETT**, RAF No.102959
E.A. **BOLSTER**, RAF No.1090706
L.P. **BOUCHER**, RAF No.177902
K.G. **BRAIN**, RAF No.171047
D.G. **BRANDRETH**, RAF No.155460
J. **BRANDT**, RAF No.39849
A.E. **BROWN**, RAF No.141474
J.M. **BRYAN**, RAF No.102570
L.A.V. **BURROWS**, RAF No.188890
A.H.O. **BUTLER**, RAF No.185370
G.S. **CHALMERS**, RAF No.131146
G.J.H. **CHRYSTALL**, RAF No.40365,
NEW ZEALAND
C.A.G. **CLARK**, RAF No.42192,
SOUTH AFRICA

G.R.J. **CLARKE**, RAF No.1317253
G. **CLUBLEY**, RAF No.174702
H.StJ. **COGHLAN**, AAF No.90117
M.J.B. **COLE**, RAF No.156033
J.D. **COUPLAND**, RAF No.55038, *CANADA*
A.V. **CRORY**, RAF No.1576679
J.R. **CROSSLEY**, RAF No.100647
J.A. **CUNNINGHAM**, RAF No.197815
R.O. **CURTIS**, RAF No.63456
I.J. **DAVIES**, RAF No.63418
J.T. **DAVIDSON**, RAF No.114477
J.R.D. **DENNEHEY**, RAF No.102538
A.I. **DOIG**, RAF No.565067
N. **DUGDALE**, RAF No.131147
R.J. **EASTABROOK**, RAF No.1339249
F.A. **EDWARDS**, RAF No.1604041
A.C.S. **ENSELL**, RAF No.139035
D.G. **EVANS**, RAF No.164918, *CANADA*
H.G. **EVANS**, RAF No.1535086
W.J. **EVANS**, RAF No.?
J.A. **FORREST**, RAF No.187680
F.M. **FURBER**, RAF No.80203, *RHODESIA*
D.W. **GUTTRIDGE**, RAF No.150045
A.R. **HACK**, RAF No.1388930
J.M. **HADOW**, RAF No.122121
R.O.G. **HÄGGBERG**, RAF No.120677, *SWEDEN*
O. **HARRIS**, RAF .?
A. **HAWKER**, RAF No.135734
J.A. **HAYNES**, RAF No.547410
D.E. **HELMORE**, RAF No.1322888
J. **HODGSON**, RAF No.?
J.W.E. **HOLMES**, RAF No.114491
W.A. **HOWELL**, RAF No.37601
J.G. **HUGUES**, RAF No.41706
F.W. **HUMPHREYS**, RAF No.?
L.G.R. **HUTT**, RAF No.137438
A.C. **JONAS**, RAF No.125528
D.StJ. **JOWITT**, RAF No.114169
D.T.N. **KELLY**, RAF No.124453
O.R. **KELSICK**, RAF No.149954
D. **KENYON**, RAF No.?
J.M. **KEY**, RAF No.128878
H.C. **KNIGHT**, RAF No.80270, *SOUTH AFRICA*
R.S. **KNIGHT-CLARKE**, RAF No.1382060
J.C. **LADD**, RAF No.?

P.M. **LA GETTE**, RAF No.107776, *USA*
P.A. **LANGLEY**, RAF No.1804392
J.C. **LAWTON**, RAF No.65584
J. **LONDON**, RAF No.115148
J.F. **LUING**, RAF No.121527
D.O. **LUKE**, RAF No.124524
J. **MADDOCKS**, RAF No.51271
W. **MALIA**, RAF No.?
G. **MARSLAND**, RAF No.41940
G.W. **MARTIN**, RAF No.102619
D. **MURRAY**, RAF No.119128
H.T. **NICHOLLS**, RAF No.174073
R.A. **NICKLESS**, RAF No.1315591
J.H. **NUTTER**, RAF No.1450367
D.B. **OGILVIE**, RAF No.83287
H.L. **O'NEIL**, RAF No.53988
J.A.H.G. **PENNANT**, RAF No.1387662
C.G. **POINTS**, RAF No.655554
C. **PEIRSON-JONES**, RAF No.162846
M. **PESKETT**, RAF No.?
T.J. **PIKE**, RAF No.1316008
J.W.T. **PURDY**, RAF No.169567
H.W. **RAMSEY**, RAF No.571776
K.H. **REEVE**, RAF No.165613
B.L. **ROBERTSON**, RAF No.748333
D.A. **SAMANT**, RAF No.108957, *INDIA*
J. **SAMPLE**, AAF No.90278
J.A.W. **SANDY**, RAF No.116508
J.A.D. **SHEMELD**, RAF No.185729
R.E.G. **SHEWARD**, RAF No.120531,
ARGENTINA
A. **SIBBALD**, RAF No.1343164
A.C. **SMITH**, RAF No.156929
R.L. **SMITH**, RAF No.129958
B. **SOULSBY**, RAF No.126629
L.A. **SPENCER**, RAF No.?
T.A. **SUTHERLAND**, RAF No.655932
J.A. **STEPHEN**, RAF No.55561
C.H. **STONE**, RAF No.113862
P.E. **TICKNER**, RAF No.121411
A. **TORRANCE**, RAF No.64932
P.H.B. **UNWIN**, RAF No.111127
J.E. **VAN SCHAICK**, RAF No.114086
F.G. **WALDRON**, RAF No.1277168
G.O.H. **WALKER**, RAF No.1382117

L. **Walker**, RAF .?
P.T. **Ward**, RAF No.45608
S.C. **Webb**, RAF .?
R.O. **Westlake**, RAF No.924127
T.A. **Willis**, RAF No.198717
A. **Witham**, RAF No.1336599
W.G. **Wood**, RAF .?
R. **Woodhouse**, RAF .?
R.S. **Woodward**, RAF No.74698
J.B. **Wray**, RAF No.37874

RCAF

C.R. **Abbott**, Can./J.17953
J.H. **Ashton**, Can./J.17890
J.R. **Baldwin**, Can./J.25777
J.R. **Brennan**, Can./R.72637
A.G. **Brunet**, Can./J.17907
R.W. **Clarke**, Can./J.26500
J. **Colton**, Can./J.90006
J.L. **Dehoux**, Can./J.15145
C.W. **De-Shane**, Can./J.15148
A.G. **Dickson**, Can./J.26498
W.A. **Flett**, Can./J.98897
J.C. **Holder**, Can./J.25779
R.A. **Johnstone**, Can./J.22310
G.D. **Kennedy**, Can./J.27869
D.E.G. **Martyn**, Can./J.28743
J.E. **McClure**, Can./J.15505
D.B. **McPhail**, Can./R.67887
C.E. **Mercer**, Can./J.15738
L.W. **Metcalfe**, Can./J.11553
J.R. **Nixon**, Can./J.26410
M.P. **Pederson**, Can./J.85921
J.R. **Rebbetoy**, Can./J.15741
R.S. **Wilson**, Can./J.25388
M. **Wood**, Can./J.5540
R.E.D. **Wright**, Can./J.15147

RNAF

H.R. **Isachsen**, N.5453
G. **Piltingsrud**, N.1084

RNZAF

W.E.F. **Adams**, NZ413005
E.T. **Brough**, NZ412197
R.A. **Egley**, NZ421690
I.C. **Hutcheson**, NZ412694
D.A. **Roberts**, NZ411994
A.N. **Sames**, NZ411453
G.W. **Symons**, NZ412280

SAAF

N.A. **Freeman**, SAAF No.19862
A.R. **Gotze**, SAAF No.542448V
J.I.A. **Watt**, SAAF No.328515

APPENDIX IX
ROLL OF HONOUR
✝

AIRCREW

Name	Service No	Rank	Age	Origin	Date	Serial
BARCLAY, John McGowan	RAF No.655794	F/Sgt	n/k	RAF	31.07.43	KZ657
BRENNAN, John Robert	CAN./R.72637	F/Sgt	19	RCAF	27.05.42	P7122
BROWN, Alfred Edward	RAF No.141474	P/O	27	RAF	23.01.43	P7095
BURROWS, Laurence Arthur Vyvyan	RAF No.188890	P/O	23	RAF	01.01.45	JR261
BUTLER, AlexanderHugh Ormonde	RAF No.185370	P/O	23	RAF	20.09.44	PD551
CARTER, John Whitfield	AUS.412912	P/O	22	RAAF	01.04.44	MN145
CLARK, Colin Athony Gordon	RAF No.42192	F/L	28	(SA)/RAF	30.10.41	P7091
CRORY, Albert Victor	RAF No.1576679	F/Sgt	n/k	RAF	03.02.45	RB252
DAVIDSON, John Tapscott	RAF No.114577	F/O	28	RAF	14.08.43	KZ578
DEHOUX, Jospeh Laurier	CAN./J.15145	F/O	21	RCAF	02.09.43	KX698
DE-SHANE, Charles Wilbert	CAN./J.15148	P/O	20	RCAF	09.03.42	P7036
DICKSON, Hugh Gilchrist	CAN./J.26498	P/O	21	RCAF	14.09.43	KZ656
EASTABROOK, Reginald James	RAF No.1339249	F/Sgt	21	RAF	05.05.44	MM980
EDWARDS, Frederick Arthur	RAF No.1604041	Sgt	20	RAF	01.04.45	RB193
EGLEY, Richard Akehurst	NZ421690	F/O	21	RNZAF	24.03.45	RB376
FLETT, William Arthur	CAN./R.124871	W/O	n/k	RCAF	26.12.44	JP504
FREEMAN, Neville Austin	SAAF No.19962	Lt	21	SAAF	18.02.43	P7119
GUTTRIDGE, David William	RAF No.150045	F/O	27	RAF	28.09.44	MP125
HACK, Arthur Reginald	RAF No.1388930	F/Sgt	21	RAF	27.07.44	MN596
HADOW, John Maude	RAF No.122121	F/O	20	RAF	15.04.43	P7121
HÄGGBERG, Ralph Otto Gustaf	RAF No.120677	P/O	20	(SWE)/RAF	12.02.42	P7093
HAWKER, Arthur	RAF No.135734	F/O	25	RAF	21.05.44	MN312
HOLDER, James Caufiled	CAN./J.25779	F/O	22	RCAF	04.08.44	JR511
HUTCHESON, Ian Cameron	NZ412694	F/O	28	RNZAF	27.08.44	MN803
JOHNSTONE, Ralph Alexander	CAN./J.22310	F/O	22	RCAF	27.07.44	MN156
JOWITT, Douglas St-John	RAF No.114169	F/O	n/k	RAF	31.10.42	P7115
KNIGHT, Harold Crosbie	RAF No.80270	F/L	27	(SA)/RAF	21.05.44	JR433
KNIGHT-CLARKE, Robert Sutherland	RAF No.1382060	W/O	24	RAF	12.04.45	JR444
MANFRED, Noel John Marsden	AUS.417627	F/O	23	RAAF	18.11.44	MN191
MARTIN, George William	RAF No.102619	P/O	n/k	RAF	12.02.42	P7106
MERCER, Charles Eldred	CAN./J.15738	P/O	24	RCAF	18.02.43	P7114
MUSGRAVE, Edward Lancelot	AUS.403528	F/O	25	RAAF	18.05.43	P7063
NUTTER, James Henry	RAF No.1450347	F/Sgt	21	RAF	23.06.45	SW426
PENNANT, John Arthur Hugh Gerraint	RAF No.1387662	F/Sgt	23	RAF	14.04.45	MP154
PILTINGSRUD, Gunnar	N.1084	Major	33	RNAF	24.09.44	MN955
PURDY, Jack WilliamThomas	RAF No.169567	P/O	26	RAF	12.02.44	MM974
REBBETOY, James Reginald	CAN./J.15741	F/O	26	RCAF	25.04.43	P7058
ROBERTSON, Basil Lionel	RAF No.748333	W/O	20	RAF	12.02.42	P7107
SAMPLE, John	AAF No.90278	S/L	28	RAF	28.10.41	P7053
SANDY, John Anthony William	RAF No.116508	P/O	n/k	RAF	12.02.42	P7050
SHEMELD, John Albert Desmond	RAF No.185729	P/O	26	RAF	31.12.44	MN660
SOULSBY, Bernard	RAF No.126629	F/O	28	RAF	07.10.43	KZ620
WITHAM, Albert	RAF No.1336599	W/O	21	RAF	25.05.44	MN469
WOOD, Matthew	CAN./J.5540	F/L	32	RCAF	18.08.44	MN126
WRIGHT, Robert Elmer Douglas	CAN./J.15147	P/O	26	RCAF	04.05.42	P7103

Total: 45

Australia: 3, Canada: 11, New Zealand: 2, Norway: 1, South Africa: 3, Sweden :1, United Kingdom: 24

GROUNDCREW

Name	Service No	Rank	Age	Origin	Date	Serial
NORRIS, Ronald Arthur	RAF No.1871068	AC1	20	RAF	01.01.45	-

Total: 1

Above: Whirlwinds of No.137 Squadron lined up along the perimeter track at Matlask early in 1942. The nearest aircraft, SF-P/ P6982 which was issued to No.137 Sqn on 07.02.42. Earlier, between December 1940 and September 1941, it was with No.263 Sqn. After accidental damage, on 26 May 1942, it was repaired and stored at No.18 MU and was eventually scrapped in September 1944.
(J. Gates)

Left: Whirlwind P7055 served with No.137 Sqn between November 1941 and February 1943. It was issued to No.263 Sqn in June 1943, ending its career with this unit. By November 1943 it was one of the last operational Whirlwinds still in service.
(via Chris Thomas)

Below left: Taken of charge in April 1941, P6997 served in miscellaneous second line units like the AFDU and A&AEE before being issued to No.137 Sqn in January 1943. It remained in the Squadron's inventory for six months, before passing to No.263 Sqn with which it served until January 1944.
(Author's collection)

Above, one of the Squadron's Whirlwind, P7012/SF-V, is re-armed with 250-lb bombs in May 1943, shortly before being passed to the other Whirlwind squadron, No.263. By that time, the Whirlwind had become a fighter-bomber, after performing poorly as a conventional interceptor. As a fighter-bomber, the Whirlwind met with greater success. *(Author's collection).*
Below, P7037/SF-J which ended its career with No.137 Squadron after this accident in October 1942. The pilot, Desmond A. Roberts (RNZAF), escaped uninjured and after repairs the aircraft was delivered to No.263 Squadron.
(D.A. Roberts via Paul Sortehaug)

No.137's Hurricane IVs could be fitted with a pair of 40mm cannon or eight rockets. Although the latter were thought the more effective of the two options, they were unable to be used over occupied territory because the weapon was still secret. Consequently some Hurricanes remained fitted with the cannon, like SF-Y/ KZ662, which was used on No.137's first Hurricane Rhubarb on 23 July 1943. *(E. Ashworth via Rob Bowater)*

A pair of No.137's new Typhoons stationed at readiness at the end of Lympne's snow-covered runway, during the second week of February 1944. SF-Z/ JR504 was later transferred to No.56 Squadron in exchange for an RP-capable aircraft. SF-R/ MM974, would be the squadron's first Typhoon casualty when lost, along with it's pilot, attacking a Noball site on 12th February 1944. *(L.P. Boucher)*

No.124 Wing's maintenance area, at B.58 Melsbroek, features elaborately camouflaged hangars, previously occupied by the Luftwaffe. Typhoon SF-N/ MN627, was one of No.137 Squadron's most successful aircraft in the anti-Diver operations - with four destroyed to its credit; however it was lost in action shortly after this photograph was taken, after being hit by flak on 30 September 1944. The pilot, W/O Mark Whitby (RAAF), managed to force-land southwest of Nijmegan in Allied territory; the aircraft was beyond repair. See colour profile. *(IWM)*
Usually flown by Pilot Officer Edwin Ashworth, MN995/SF-X taking off from B-78 Eindhoven with its rockets under the wings. By the end of the month, it was lost to flak. See colour profile for further details. *(AWM)*

Above: MN134/SF-S armed and ready for another mission over Germany during October 1944. This machine was usually flown by 'B' Flight Commander's Douglas G. Brandbreth, who had previously flown with No.181 Sqn, with whom he was received his DFC. This Typhoon had recently returned to the squadron after an accident that had occurred on 26 September, and the serial was overpainted at this time. See colour profile for further details. *(AWM)*
Below, Another Typhoon, MN660/SF-K, which was lost in action, when attacking a train, on 31 December 1944. The aircraft was shot down in flames by flak, P/O James Shemeld, the pilot, being killed. This aircraft had been issued to No.137 Sqn early the previous September. *(IWM)*

Left: Flying Officer Ken Brain awaits the signal to start up his Typhoon SF-R/ PD611, at B-78 Eindhoven, 15 December 1944. The Typhoon carries two rockets and a 44-gallon tank under each wing, for a long-range 'armed recce' into Germany. See colour profile. *(P.E. Tickner)*

Left: Hawker Typhoon Mk.IB, MN374/SF-X, being checked or warmed-up for a flight in January 1945. It was regularly flown by Flight Sergeant John A.H.G. 'Johnny' Pennant. See colour profile. *(IWM)*
Below: Taken during spring 1945, this photo shows an early Typhoon production model with a small tailplane, and a 3-blade propeller. Although the serial cannot be clearly read, it is believed that it is EK270. *(AWM)*

No.137 Squadron pilots at Eindhoven (B78) on 23 December 1944.
Front row, Left to Right: Edwin Ashworth, Peter Tickner, S/L Erle T. Brough (RNZAF), the Commanding Officer, John Crossley (shot down and made a PoW six days later), Michael J.B. Cole.
Middle row: Martin Peder Pederson (RCAF), 'Paddy' Crory (†03.02.45), 'Hank' Nixon (RCAF), 'Ken' Brain, 'Paddy' Shemeld (†31.12.44), George Martyn (RCAF), 'Bert' Gotze (SAAF, later with No.2 SAAF in Korea and retiring as a Brigadier General), Norman Swift (RAAF) and Arthur Burrows (†01.01.45).
Back row: 'Dick' Egley (RNZAF, †24.03.45), Gilbert Symons (RNZAF), Thomas Pike, John Horne (RAAF), John Pennant, John Colton (RCAF) and Robert Baldwin (RCAF).
Below: Informal group portrait of squadron pilots, resting outside their huts between operations, March 1945: Left to right: Sergeant Hodgson, Pilot Officer 'Will' Collins (RAAF) Pilot Officer 'Jack' Forest, Pilot Officer Geoffrey Sheldon (RAAF), Squadron Leader Ronald Barraclough, the Squadron's Commanding Officer, Captain 'Buster' Watt (SAAF). *(AWM)*

Left: Squadron Leader John Sample DFC was the first Commanding Officer of No.137 Squadron, but sadly for a short time. A Pre-war Auxiliary Air Force officer he had wide-spread experience in both the Battle of France and the Battle of Britain, and was credited with three victories.
(Andrew Thomas)

Right: Another pre-war Auxiliary Air Force officer was Humprey Coglhan, who came from No.263 Sqn, in which he had served since May 1941. He had flown in No.600 Sqn, Auxiliary Air Force before the war, having been commissioned in March 1935. In April 1937 he resigned his commission, but was recalled later for active service and returned to No.600 Sqn, prior to becoming a Whirlwind pilot. He was awarded the DFC with No.263 Sqn.
(Author's collection)

Below, three Squadron's Commanders during the Typhoon era.
Left, the Norwegian Gunnar Pilitingsrud, who was in charge of the Squadron during the critical weeks around D-Day. He was killed in action on 24 September 1944, engaged on his 52nd operational sortie with the squadron. He was the sole squadron commander to be killed in action and was succeeded by a New Zealander, Erle Brough. Brough began his operational career in April 1942 with No.132 Sqn, before sailing for Malta where he fought with Nos.603 and 229 Sqns in sequence. In August 1943 he returned to the front line for another tour, firstly with No.182 Sqn, a Typhoon unit, then No.137 Sqn until his tour expired at the end of 1944 when he was repatriated to New Zealand. The last officer who led the Squadron was Squadron Leader 'Slug' Murray who had served with No.26 Sqn during his first tour. He became a Typhoon pilot in September 1944 when he joined No.181 Sqn, then No.182 Sqn and eventually No.137 Sqn in March 1945. He left the RAF on 4 September 1946 and in 1947 made deliveries of Spitfires to the Middle East, before his untimely death in a motor accident near High Wycombe on 16 November 1947.
(Rob Bowater - Paul Sortehaug - Terry Spencer)

Clockwise, some of No.137 Sqn's personalities during the first two years:

Left, the Australian John Gates (PoW 05.12.44) posing in front of his Hurricane, the South African Neville Freeman (†18.02.43), Herbert Turner, one of the 1,500 New Zealanders who enlisted in the RAAF during the war, Dattatraya Samant of India, and of Indian parentage, the Englishman Douglas Jowitt, unique in having flown over 500 hours on Whirlwinds (†31.10.42), Paul La Gette, a Californian boy and one of a handful of Americans who flew the Whirlwind, Ralph Häggberg from Sweden, one of the few Swedes who enlisted in the RAF during the war (†12.02.42), and Desmond Roberts of New Zealand seated in his Whirlwind.
(Author's, John Gates, Chris Thomas, Paul Sortehaug)

Below: Two DFC holders, who received their awards serving with the squadron. On the left the Australian Edward Musgrave, who was killed in action on 17.05.43. On the right, the Englishman John M. Bryan, who gained the only DFC & Bar awarded to the squadron. He was later destined to lead No.198 Sqn, flying Typhoons, and became WingCo of No.136 Wing. He was killed in action on 10.06.44 at 21.
(Author's and Chris Thomas)

"COMRADES IN ARMS"

Above and below: Three Australian Typhoon pilots, all from New South Wales, in 1945. Flight Commander 'Jack' Rendal, who also flew with No.181 Sqn, with which he was awarded the DFC, Mark Whitby, who received a DFC in July 1945 for his activities with the squadron, and 'Will' Collins seated in his aircraft.
(All AWM)

Above: John Colton, a Scottish-born Canadian, one of the 15 Typhoon pilots from Canada who flew with No.137 Sqn during 1944 -1945. They suffered a rather high loss rate, with 25 percent of the total squadron casualties.
(John Colton)

Below: As with all RAF Squadrons during the war, pilots came from the all parts of the Empire, but No.137 Sqn in particular could boast that almost half of its pilots originated from the Dominions, especially during the Typhoon era. The Canadians contributed the bulk of these between 1943-1945. From left to right, Matthew Wood, a Canadian from British Columbia, killed in action on 18.08.44, Arthur Sames, a New Zealander the squadron's only V-1 ace, wearing his DFC ribbon he won while flying with No.486 (NZ) Sqn, at the far right, Ian Hutcheson, another New Zealander who was killed in action on 27.08.44.
(Paul Sortehaug)

Above and and left: One of the 15 Canadians who flew with No.137 Sqn, John Ridgeway 'Hank' Nixon. Born in Toronto, Ontario in July 1922, he enlisted in February 1942 and was trained in Canada. He received his Pilot Flying badge in May 1943 and was commissioned in the same time. Posted overseas, he arrived in UK in July the same year. Between August and November 1943 he served with No.401 (RCAF) Sqn, flying Spitfires. He then flew various second line units during the next months before being posted to No.137 Sqn early in October 1944. On 4 April 1945, he was obliged to make a force-landing and was injured while taking part of an armed recce (see operational losses). He later recalled:

'I was hit by German flak, on my 63rd operational trip, April 4, 1945. On returning to base at Eindhoven the engine of my aircraft quit. I was forced to land in a clearing in the Hochwald Forest in Germany, where my aircraft hit an anti-tank ditch and cart wheeled. The landing was okay until I hit the anti–tank ditch. The aircraft was demolished, both wings and the tail assembly immediately behind the cockpit were broken off. The engine and myself were hurdled on until I landed upside down with my left arm pinned under the aircraft. My right side was badly hurt, namely my ankle, knee, shoulder, head and broken ribs. I was knocked out. On coming to I could not get out of my seat as my arm was pinned under the aircraft. I had my revolver out ready to sever my arm as petrol was dripping close to the hot engine. However, three Flemish nurses, who were traveling on a nearby road, came to my assistance, but could not take what was left of the aircraft off my arm. Finally a Canadian Army Intelligence Officer, who was passing by in a jeep came to my rescue. With the help of the nurses and a jack in the jeep they finally got me out. He drove me to a nearby hospital on one of the wings of the aircraft make shifted into a stretcher. The hospital had been evacuated by the Germans on the previous day when the allies had passed through on their way to crossing the Rhine. The hospital was staffed by a doctor, a nurse and 3 orderlies. I was their first patient. The significant equipment in the hospital had been destroyed by the Germans. However, the doctor did have sulpha to treat my arm, but was unable to treat further injuries on my right side. A week later I was transferred to the hospital on Lady Astor's estate at Cliveden, England. After a month I was sent home on a hospital ship, the Landovery Castle, to Halifax, Canada. It was exactly 2 years from the date I had landed in England from Halifax. I was sent to Christie Street Hospital, the Veterans' Hospital in Toronto, as an outpatient until February 1946 when I was discharged from the Air Force.'

(photos and recollection provided by 'Hank' Nixon's family)

Two rare colour photos of No.137 Sqn Typhoons, taken in June 1945 whilst stationned at B-160 Kastrup in Denmark.
(via Chris Thomas)

SUMMARY OF THE OPERATIONAL ACTIVITY
No.137 Squadron

A/C types	First sortie	Last sortie	Total sorties	Tot Sub-type	Lost Ops	Lost Acc	A/C Total	Claims	V-1	Pilot †	PoWs	Eva.
WHIRLWIND I	24.10.41	21.06.43	2,223	2,223	22	8	30	4.0	-	16	3	-
HURRICANE IV	23.07.43	31.12.43	274	274	5	1	6	-	-	5	-	-
TYPHOON I	08.02.44	04.05.45	3,661	3,661	39	9	48	1.0	30.0	24	5	1
Others												
MAGISTER	-	-	-	-	-	1	1	-	-	-	-	-
HURRICANE I	-	-	-	-	1	-	1	-	-	-	-	-
OTHER CAUSES	-	-	-	-	-	-	-	-	-	-	-	-
COMPILATION	24.10.41	04.05.45		6,158	67	19	86	5.0	30.0	45	8	1

MAIN AWARDS

DSO: -

DFC: 12
including 1 Bar

DFM: 1

Points of interest :
- One of two operational Whirlwind squadrons.

Unsolved mystery
Service numbers of some pilots (see nominal roll).

Statistics :
- Lost one aircraft every 93 sorties (Whirlwind: 101 - Hurricane IV: 54.8 - Typhoon: 93.9).
- 17.50 % of the combat aircraft losses until VE-Day occured during non operational flights.

BADGE
A horse's head couped

The horse's head associates the squadron with Kent from where it flew many of its operations and the black and white markings indicates day and night.

MOTTO
DO RIGHT FEAR NAUGHT

Authority: King George VI, October 1944.

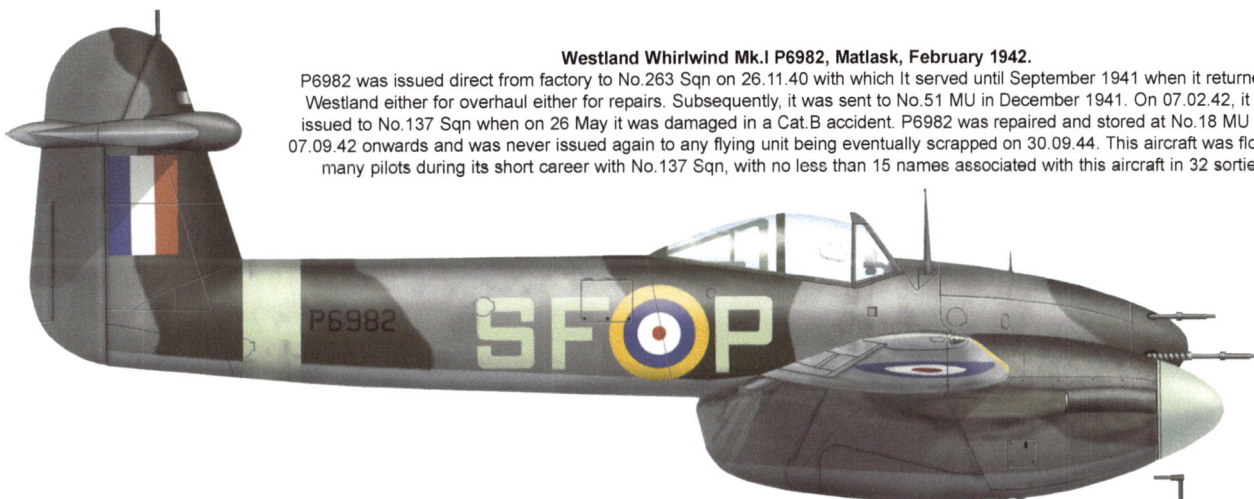

Westland Whirlwind Mk.I P6982, Matlask, February 1942.
P6982 was issued direct from factory to No.263 Sqn on 26.11.40 with which It served until September 1941 when it returned to Westland either for overhaul either for repairs. Subsequently, it was sent to No.51 MU in December 1941. On 07.02.42, it was issued to No.137 Sqn when on 26 May it was damaged in a Cat.B accident. P6982 was repaired and stored at No.18 MU from 07.09.42 onwards and was never issued again to any flying unit being eventually scrapped on 30.09.44. This aircraft was flown by many pilots during its short career with No.137 Sqn, with no less than 15 names associated with this aircraft in 32 sorties.

Westland Whirlwind Mk.I P7101, Matlask, Flight Lieutenant Leonard 'Red' Bartlett, June 1942.
Taken on charge 07.08.41, P7101 was first stored at No.18 MU before being issued to No.137 Sqn on 18.04.42 to become the mount of 'Red' Bartlett, the A Flight Commander. On 30ᵗʰ June, P7101 was hit by Lysander N1249 whilst parked. First categorised Cat.B, it was altered to Cat.E on 13ᵗʰ July. At that time it had flown 48 sorties with No.137 Sqn, mostly with Bartlett in command. 'Red' Bartlett left the squadron in September 1942 to become CO of No.253 Sqn. He survived the war and remained with the RAF retiring as a Group Captain in 1966.

Hawker Hurricane Mk.IV KZ662, Southend, Summer 1943.

The Hurricane Mk.IV had a short career with the RAF in Europe, and few missions were flown on this type. KZ662 is not exception, having flown only four operational flights, two of them with P/O 'Dave' Davidson before he was killed in August 1943 flying another Hurricane. KZ662 was taken on charge on 21 April 1943 at No.44 MU and was issued to No.137 Sqn on 22 June. It was sent to No.41 OTU on 15 February 1944 when the squadron was converted onto Typhoons. Stored, it was never issued to any flying unit until being struck off charge after the war.

Hawker Hurricane Mk.I V7752, Manston, Spring 1944.

This Hurricane had a long career with the RAF. Taken on charge on 7 December 1940, it first served with No.96 Sqn but for a short time only, early in 1941. From then, it served at various training and miscellaneous units. At a later stage it served as a communication aircraft with No.263 Sqn before being issued to the squadron on 20 January 1944 for the same purpose and received a question mark as individual marking. It later received full D-Day markings and was eventually destroyed on the ground on 1 January 1945 during Operation 'Bodenplatte'.

Hawker Typhoon Mk.IB JR535, Flight Lieutenant Ronald E.G. Sheward (Argentina), Colerne, January 1944.

Taken on charge on 25 December 1943, JR535 was delivered to No.137 Squadron on 4 January 1944 as one of it's initial complement of Typhoons, and had a small tailplane and a 3-blade propeller. JR535 'SF-B' was allocated to F/L 'Ronnie' Sheward 'A' Flight commander. Initially JR535 had Typhoon identity stripes under the wings, as shown here, but these were removed on 7 February 1944. At the end of March it was one of 12 aircraft exchanged for slightly newer No.56 Squadron Typhoons (which were RP-capable). Sheward's new 'B' from No.56 Squadron was MN145. 'Ronnie' Sheward, also known as 'Shewie' or 'Bentos', was a British Argentinian who had earlier flown Spitfires and Hurricanes with No.164 (Argentine-British) Squadron and, on his second tour, would command 'B' Flight No.263 Squadron before being promoted to command No.266 (Rhodesia) Squadron.

Hawker Typhoon Mk.IB MM972, Warrant Officer John Gates (RAAF), Lympne, March 1944.

One of the first Typhoons off the production line with RP fittings, this aircraft arrived with 137 Sqn on 14 January 1944, becoming SF-F. It is shown as it appeared from mid February to March 1944. it was flown by W/O J.Gates on Ramrod escorts during the latter month. On 25 March 1944 MM972 suffered an engine failure and F/O B.W.Gutteridge made a forced landing at St Mary's in the Marsh near Dymchurch. Gutteridge was uninjured but the aircraft was 'category E' – a write-off. Many of 137 Squadron's Typhoons carried a repeat of the aircraft's individual letter on the leading edge of the wings, between the cannons and fuselage. Where this feature is visible in reference photos of the above subjects, a 'scrap view' has been used to illustrate the feature. It is very likely that the letter was displayed on both wings; colours appear to have been white or yellow.

Hawker Typhoon Mk.IB MN429, Manston, July 1944.

When MN145 failed to return from a shipping patrol on 1 April 1944, F/L Sheward received MN429 as his new 'B' on 10 April, but only flew it on 3 operational sorties before he was posted to 3 TEU as an instructor. MN429 was flown by many different pilots thereafter, including W/O J.A.Horne, RAAF, who shared the destruction of a V-1 in this aircraft on 28 June 1944. On 10 July 1944, when flown by P/O Martin Pedersen, RCAF, MN429's port tyre burst on take-off and the undercarriage collapsed on landing at Manston. After factory repair the aircraft saw no further operational service. MN429 is shown here with full 'D-Day stripes' which it still carried during the first week of July 1944. It is not known for certain whether the code letter on the fuselage was painted out as shown here but seems likely as other aircraft in the unit carried temporary code letters on the tail, as illustrated. It had a large tailplane and a 3-blade propeller. Note the individual letter painted on the leading edge.

Hawker Typhoon Mk.IB MN627, B-48 Amiens-Glisy, France, September 1944.

Taken on charge on 2 May 1944 MN627 became SF-N when it arrived at No.137 Sqn on 26 May. It was then flown by various 'B' Flight pilots. During the 'anti-Diver' campaign it was responsible for the the destruction of 4 V-1s, including 2 on 7 July 1944, when flown by F/O James C. Holder (RCAF). On 30 September 1944 MN627 was hit by flak but W/O Mark J.Whitby (RAAF) managed to force-land southwest of Nijmegan in Allied territory; the aircraft was beyond repair. MN627 is shown here as it appeared early in September, the 'D-Day stripes' having been removed from the top surfaces of the wings and from the fuselage upper surfaces as far down as the bottom of the code letters. It had a large tailplane and a 4-blade propeller.

Hawker Typhoon Mk.IB MN134, Flight Lieutenant Douglas G. Brandreth, B-78 Eindhoven, Netherlands, October 1944.

Originally coded SF-N when taken on charge on 3 March 1944, MN134 was recoded as SF-S when taken over by the new 'B' Flight commander F/L D.G.Brandreth early in May. This aircraft was particularly successful against the V-1s with 9 destroyed although Brandreth only claimed one in this aircraft. On 26 September 1944 F/O Hans Isachsen (Nor) landed in MN134 with the tail wheel not fully extended; the damage was repaired by 403 R&SU and included a repaint of the rear fuselage which covered the aircraft serial number – as depicted above when it returned to the squadron at the beginning of October. At the end of the month Brandreth finished his tour and was posted to 83 GSU as an instructor and returned to his first unit, No.181 Sqn in June 1945 with which he had served in 1943. Note the individual letter painted on the leading edge.

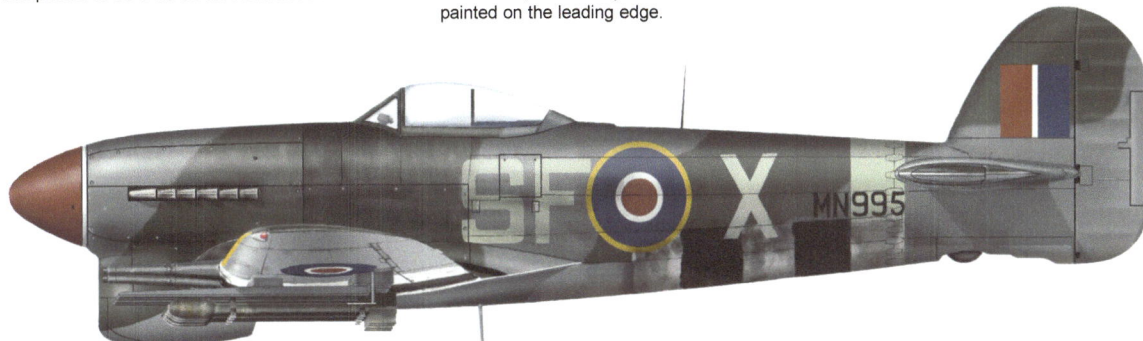

Hawker Typhoon Mk.IB MN995, Pilot Officer Edwin Ashworth, B-78 Eindhoven, Netherlands, October 1944.

Taken on charge on 15 July 1943, it was stored until being issued to with No.137 Sqn on 20 August 1944 when it is believed to have been coded SF-C. By early October it had become SF-X and was often flown by P/O Edwin Ashworth who had arrived on the squadron as it changed from Whirlwinds to Hurricanes; his tour would expire on 5 January 1945, but not before he had a close call on 29 October. MN995 was hit by flak and he was obliged to bale out over the front lines near Roermond but was fortunately rescued by the crew of the Forward Control Post. This Typhoon was equipped with a large tailplane and a 4-blade propeller.

Hawker Typhoon Mk.IB PD611, Pilot Officer Kenneth G. Brain, B-86 Helmond, Netherlands, January 1945.

PD611 was taken on charge on 20 September 1944 and was issued to No.124 Wing on 20 November before being eventually taken on charge by No.137 Sqn by 14 December 1944 becoming the new SF-R, P/O 'Ken' Brain's aircraft (replacing JP504 which then became SF-E). It was built with a large tailplane and was equipped with a 4-blade propeller and a tropical air filter. It is seen here fitted with 44-gallon drop tanks and reduced RP load, for long-range intruder sorties into Germany, in search of rail traffic. It remained his aircraft until he finished his tour at Warmwell APC in March 1945. PD611 survived the hostilities and was still with No.137 Sqn when it was renamed No.174 Sqn at Warmwell on 26 August 1945. On the same day it was damaged in a cross-wind landing, when the undercarriage collapsed. A team from No.67 MU commenced a 'repair on site' but by 14 November PD611 had been declared 'Category E'.

Hawker Typhoon Mk.IB MN374, Flight Sergeant John A.H.G. 'Johnny' Pennant, B-86 Helmond, Netherlands, January 1945.

MN374 was taken on charge on 1 March 1944 and served at first with No.193 Sqn as DP-H and following a damage from a Bf109 on 29 June 1944, MN374 was repaired and eventually issued to 83 GSU on 5 December. One of the replacements for No.124 Wing's Bodenplatte losses, MN374 was with No.137 Sqn by 4 January 1945, becoming SF-X when MN995 was lost the next day. Throughout February MN374 as flown by F/Sgt 'Johnny' Pennant who was killed in action on 14 April 1945, the last squadron's war casualty. It was unusually marked in that the canopy framing was painted black. It appears that the aircraft was damaged while the unit was attending the APC at Warmwell, between 9 and 18 March. With the end of hostilities, Typhoon repairs were cancelled and MN374 was SOC on 17 May 1945. It had a large tailplane and a 3-blade propeller.

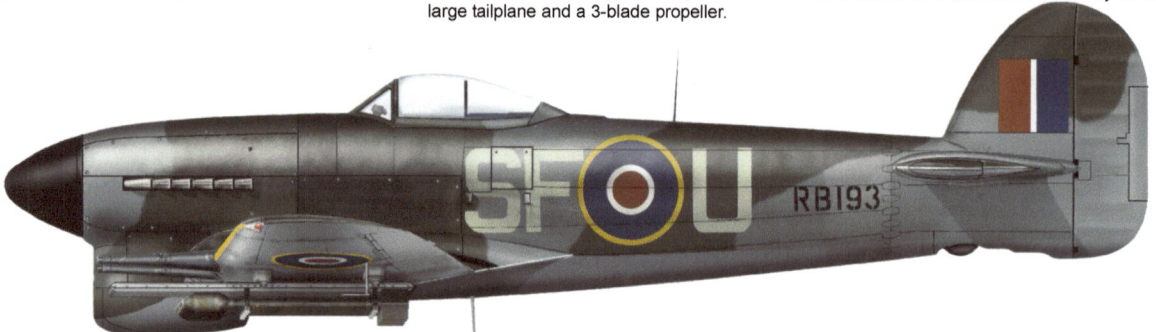

Hawker Typhoon Mk.IB RB193, Flying Officer Donald E.G. Martyn (RCAF), B-86 Helmond, Netherlands, March 1945.

RB193 was taken on charge on 20 September 1944 and after service with No.182 Sqn, between November 1944 and January 1945, RB193 was transferred to No.137 Sqn early in February and coded SF-U. It was normally flown by F/O Donald Martyn and although damaged during anti-flak operations during the Rhine crossings was soon back in service. However on 1 April 1945 it was hit by flak again but Sgt Frederick A. Edwards did not survive the subsequent forced landing east of Munster. It had been buit with a large tailplane and a 4-blade propeller and a tropical air filter had been installed.

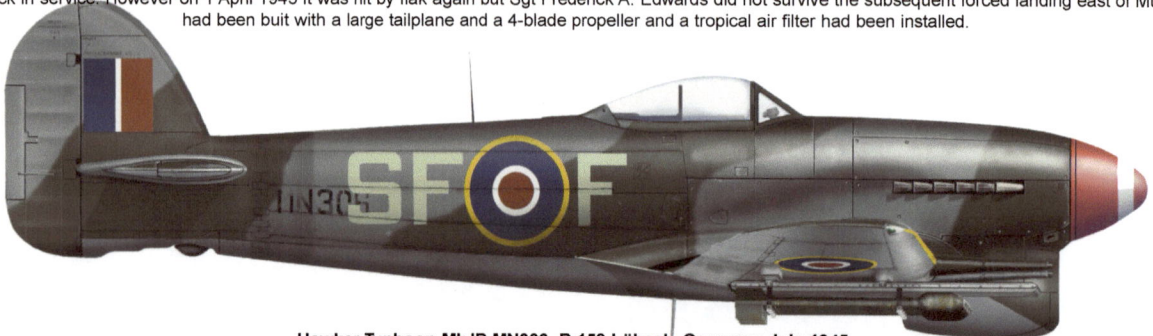

Hawker Typhoon Mk.IB MN306, B-158 Lübeck, Germany, July 1945.

Following service with No.183 Sqn which terminated on Christmas Day 1944 MN306 went to No.403 R&SU for repair; by 5 January MN306 was with No.137 Sqn and was coded SF-F. It was usually flown by F/O Michael J.B.Cole until early February when P/O Mark J. Whitby (RAAF) became its usual pilot. Receiving damage on 22 March MN306 was repaired and on return to No.137 Sqn was now usually flown by F/Sgt G.R.J.Clarke. Surviving the hostilities MN306 was still with No.137 Sqn when it was disbanded by renumbering the unit No.174 Sqn on 26 August 1945. It was still wearing No.137's markings (including its peacetime red and white spinner) when it was written off in a forced landing NW of Oldenburg on 12 September 1945. Note non-standard camouflage pattern on rear fuselage. It had a small tailplane and a 3-blade propeller.